T0268852

SPANISH-ENGLISH
ENGLISH-SPANISH
Compact Dictionary

SPANISH-ENGLISH
ENGLISH-SPANISH
Compact Dictionary

Ila Warner

HIPPOCRENE BOOKS, INC.
New York

For information, address:
HIPPOCRENE BOOKS, INC.
171 Madison Ave.
New York, NY 10016
www.hippocrenebooks.com

Library of Congress Cataloging-in-Publication Data
Warner, Ila.
   Spanish-English, English-Spanish compact dictionary
   / Ila Warner.
     p. cm.
   ISBN-13: 978-0-7818-1041-8
   ISBN-10: 0-7818-1041-8
   1. Spanish language--Dictionaries--English.
2. English language--Dictionaries--Spanish. I. Title.

PC4640.W37 2004
463'.21--dc22

                         2004047581

Printed in the United States of America.

CONTENTS

A BRIEF GUIDE TO SPANISH PRONUNCIATION

This dictionary and phrasebook provides a phonetic pronunciation for all vocabulary and phrases. However, as many English-speaking people have studied Spanish at some time in their lives and as the Spanish sound system is relatively simple, a review of the rules of pronunciation may be all that some people require.

There are, of course, variations in the pronunciation of Spanish from one Latin American country to another. The pronunciation provided in this book is what is considered standard Latin American pronunciation.

Vowels

The pronunciation of the Spanish vowels is much simpler than the pronunciation of

English vowels, as each vowel has only one sound. An English vowel, in contrast, can have from five to seven different sounds.

The Spanish vowel sounds are as follows:

A	The sound of <u>a</u> in "father"
E	The sound of <u>a</u> in "date"
I	The sound of <u>ee</u> in "meet"
O	The sound of <u>o</u> in "go"
U	The sound of <u>o</u> in "who"

Diphthongs

A diphthong is a combination of a weak and a strong vowel pronounced together in the same syllable. The following are the more common diphthongs with their pronunciation:

AI	The sound of <u>i</u> in "side"
AU	The sound of <u>ow</u> in "cow"
EI	The sound of <u>ay</u> in "say"
IA	The sound of <u>ya</u> in "yard"
IE	The sound of <u>ye</u> in "yet"
OI	The sound of <u>oy</u> in "boy"

Consonants

Only a limited number of Spanish consonants present problems in pronunciation. The rest are either identical to English or very similar. The following are the ones that require special attention:

B and V   Both are pronounced alike, but each have two different pronunciations depending on where they fall in a word or sentence. B or V at the beginning of a sentence or phrase is pronounced like the B in "bed." B or V between vowels has a soft sound, more like the English V.

C   Sounds like S before E and I. Sounds like K before A, O and U.

G   Sounds like the English H before E and I.

H   Always silent.

J   Similar to the English H.

LL   Like the Y in "yes."

Ñ	Like the NY in "canyon."
Q	Q is always followed by a U in Spanish and is pronounced like the English K.
X	Before a consonant, it sounds like the English S.
	Before a vowel, like the English word "eggs."
Z	Like the English S.
W and K	These letters are not a part of the Spanish alphabet and are only found in certain foreign words.

Stress

In Spanish the stress falls naturally on the next-to-last syllable in words ending in a vowel, *n* or *s*. If a word ends in a consonant other than *n* or *s*, the stress falls on the last syllable. Exceptions to the above rules are indicated by an accent over the stressed syllable.

A Brief Overview of Spanish Grammar

The casual traveler to Latin America is not likely to master Spanish grammar in the period immediately before or during the trip. Thus, it is beyond the scope of this book to delve into its complexities. However, it is very useful to have certain notions of its structure. The following outline should be helpful.

Nouns

In Spanish, every noun is either masculine or feminine. Typically nouns ending in *o* are masculine and nouns ending in *a* are feminine. The gender of nouns that end in some other letter simply must be learned. The gender of nouns is indicated by the articles used with them. The definite article "the" in Spanish has four forms, masculine singular *el*, masculine plural *los*, feminine singular *la* and feminine plural *las*.

Singular

el libro   the book
(el LEE-broh)

la mesa   the table
(lah MAY-say)

Plural

los libros   the books
(lohs LEE-brohs)

las mesas   the tables
(lahs MAY-sahs)

The English articles "a" and "an" are *un* (masculine) and *una* (feminine) in Spanish.

un libro   a book
(oon LEE-broh)

una mesa   a table
(OO-nah MAY-sah)

When *un* is pluralized to *unos* and *una* to *unas*, the meaning is "some."

unos libros   some books
(OO-nohs LEE-brohs)

unas mesas   some tables
(OO-nahs MAY-sahs)

It is very easy to make Spanish nouns plural. The rule is that you add *s* to any noun ending in a vowel and *es* to any noun ending in a consonant.

boleto	ticket	*boletos*	tickets
(boh-LAY-toh)		(boh-LAY-tohs)	
tren	train	*trenes*	trains
(trayn)		(TRAY-nays)	

Adjectives

In Spanish, adjectives—those words that either limit or describe nouns—agree with the nouns they modify in both gender and number. This is somewhat difficult to master but fortunately errors in agreement rarely stand in the way of understanding.

It is important, though, to know that descriptive adjectives usually follow the noun in Spanish rather than precede it as they do in English. So while English-speakers say "red dress," Spanish-speakers will say "dress red," (*vestido rojo*, bays-TEE-doh ROH-hoh).

Possessive adjectives are a special type of adjective that—as the name implies—shows possession. They are the Spanish forms of "our", "my", "his", "their", etc.

Singular	Plural		
mi (mee)	my	*mis* (mees)	my
su (soo)	his/her/ your	*sus* (soos)	their/your
nuestro (noo-AYS-troh)	our (m)	*nuestros* (noo-AYS-trohs)	our (m)
nuestra (noo-AYS-trah)	our (f)	*nuestras* (noo-AYS-trahs)	our (f)

These adjectives agree with the thing possessed rather than with the possessor. Thus "my books" is not *mi libros*, but rather *mis libros*.

It should be noted that the possession of a noun by another noun is indicated differently in Spanish than it is in English, which uses "'s" or "s'" to show possession. Possession in Spanish is indicated by using the preposition *de* followed by the possessor. So in Spanish, "Alfred's letter" would be "the letter of Alfred," *la carta de Alfredo*. When the article *el* follows the preposition *de*, it contracts to *del*. Therefore, the "taxi door" ("the door of the taxi") becomes *la puerta del taxi*.

Demonstrative adjectives—so called because they demonstrate or point out— are still another special type of adjective. They are the equivalent of our "this," "that," "these" and "those." There are two forms for "that" and "those" in Spanish, one that points out something near the person spoken to and the other, to something distant from both the person speaking and the person spoken to.

These forms are as follows:

MASCULINE FEMININE
Singular

este	*esta*	this (<u>noun</u>)
(ESS-tay)	(ESS-tah)	(near speaker)
ese	*esa*	that (<u>noun</u>)
(ESS-say)	(ESS-sah)	(near person spoken to)
aquel	*aquella*	that (<u>noun</u>)
(ah-KAYL)	(ah-KAY-yah)	(distant from both)

Plural

estos	*estas*	these (<u>noun</u>)
(ESS-tohs)	(ESS-tahs)	(near speaker)
esos	*esas*	those (<u>noun</u>)
(ESS-ohs)	(ESS-ahs)	(near person spoken to)

| *aquellos* | *aquellas* | those (<u>noun</u>) |
| (ah-KAY-yohs) | (ah-KAY-yahs) | (distant from both) |

Pronouns

The pronouns used as the subjects of sentences are as follows:

Singular		**Plural**	
yo	I	*nosotros/ as*	we
(yoh)		(noh-SOH-trohs/trahs)	
tú	you (fam.)		
(too)			
usted	you (for.)	*ustedes*	you (for.)
(oo-STAY)		(oo-STAY-days)	
él	he	*ellos*	they (masc.)
(el)		(AYH-yohs)	
ella	she	*ellas*	they (fem.)
(AY-yah)		(AY-yahs)	

As verbs in Spanish are highly inflected, the verb endings often make it clear who the subject of the sentence is. Therefore, it is not always necessary to use the subject pronouns as it is in English. If there is any confusion as to the subjects, it is always appropriate to use them.

The familiar forms for "you," *tú* (or *vos*, which is used in some parts of Central America and the Cone of South America) and *vosotros* are not included in the following section on verbs. These familiar forms are similar to the words "thee" and "thou," which have fallen out of usage in English. Though their equivalents in Spanish are commonly used, it is much safer for the traveler to use the formal *usted* and *ustedes* forms of "you" so as not to risk giving offense by appearing to be too familiar.

Other types of pronouns include the direct and indirect object pronouns. However, these are quite difficult and can be effectively avoided by simply using nouns. Rather than trying to say, "I bought them for her," just say, "I bought the magazines for Mary."

Verbs

Unquestionably, verbs are the most difficult area of Spanish grammar. The following only covers the most basic tenses of regular verbs—those verbs that follow consistent patterns throughout all tenses—and a few of the most essential irregular verbs.

In Spanish, all infinitives—the equivalent of "to" plus the verb in English as in "to read," "to play," etc.—end in *ar*, *er* or *ir*. The following are examples of regular *ar*, *er*, and *ir* verbs in the present tense:

ar **verbs** (*comprar*)

yo compro (COHM-proh)	I buy
él/ella/usted compra (COHM-prah)	he/she/you buy(s)
nosotros/ as compramos (cohm-PRAH-mohs)	we buy
ustedes compran (COHM-prahn)	they/you (plural) buy

<u>er</u> **verbs** (*vender*)

yo vendo (VAYN-doh)	I sell
él/ella/usted vende (VAYN-day)	he/she/you sell(s)
nosotros vendemos (vayn-DAY-mohs)	we sell
ellos/ellas/ ustedes venden (VAYN-dayn)	they/you (plural) sell

<u>ir</u> **verbs** (*vivir*)

yo vivo (VEE-voh)	I live
él/ella/usted vive (VEE-vay)	he/she/you live(s)
nosotros/as vivimos (vee-VEE-mohs)	we live
ellos/ellas/ ustedes viven (VEE-vayn)	they/you (plural) live

Those verbs that do not follow regular patterns throughout all tenses are called

irregular verbs and have to be learned
individually. Included here in the present
tense are a few of the commonest irregular verbs.

The **verbs** "to be"

There are two verbs "to be" in Spanish,
ser (sayr) and *estar* (ess-TAHR). *Ser* is
used to show a permanent characteristic
such as, "Snow is white," or "Manuel is
intelligent." Its forms are:

yo soy (sohy)	I am
él/ella/usted es (ess)	he/she is, you are
nosotros/as somos (SOH-mohs)	we are
ellos/ellas/ ustedes son (sohn)	they/you (plural) are

The verb *estar* is used in two ways: 1) to
indicate the location of someone or some-

thing, such as, "Cancún is in Mexico" or "The book is on the table" and 2) to describe a passing condition such as "Mother is very tired" or "Carlos is sick today." Its forms are:

yo estoy (ess-TOHY)	I am
él/ella/usted está (ess-TAH)	he/she is, you are
nosotros/as estamos (ess-TAH-mohs)	we are
ellos/ellas/ustedes están (ess-TAHN)	they/you (plural) are

The **verb** *tener*

Another very useful irregular verb is *tener* which means "to have" in the sense of "to possess." Its present tense forms are as follows:

yo tengo (TAYN-goh)	I have

16

él/ella/usted tiene (tee-AY-nay)	he/she has, you have
nosotros/as tenemos (tay-NAY-mohs)	we have
ellos/ellas/ustedes tienen (tee-AY-nayn)	they/you (plural) have

The verb *ir*, "to go" is particularly useful as the basis for forming a relatively simple substitute for the future tense. Here are its present tense forms:

The **verb** *ir*

yo voy (vohy)	I go, I'm going
él/ella/usted va (vah)	he/she goes, you go he's/she's/you're going
nosotros/as vamos (VAH-mohs)	we go, we're going
ellos/ellas/ ustedes van (vahn)	they/you go, they're/ you're (plural) going

To form the substitute for the future tense, choose the appropriate form of *ir* and follow it with the preposition *a* plus an infinitive.

Van a visitar el museo.	They're going to visit the museum.

(Vahn ah vee-see-TAHR el moo-SAY-oh.)

Voy a comer allí mañana.	I'm going to eat there tomorrow.

(Vohy ah coh-MAYR ah-EE mah-NYAN-nah.)

Past Tense

There are various verb tenses in Spanish that indicate past actions. However, only the forms of the simple past (or preterite) tense will be included here. This form is used to indicate a one-time action in the past that is over and done with, such as, "I bought a blouse yesterday" or "Juan ate in that restaurant last Sunday."

Here are the simple past tense forms of the regular verbs:

comprar (to buy)

yo compré (cohm-PRAY)	I bought
él/ella/usted compró (cohm-PROH)	he/she/you bought
nosotros/ *as compramos* (cohm-PRAH-mohs)	we bought
ellos/ellas/ustedes *compraron* (cohm-PRAH-rohn)	they/you (plural) bought

vender (to sell)

yo vendí (vayn-DEE)	I sold
él/ella/usted vendió (vayn-DYOH)	he/she/you sold
nosotros/as vendimos (vayn-DEE-mohs)	we sold
ellos/ellas/ustedes *vendieron* (vayn-dee-YEHR-ohn)	they/you (plural) sold

vivir (to live)

yo viví (vee-VEE)	I lived
él/ella/usted vivió (vee-VYOH)	he/she/you lived
nosotros/as vivimos (vee-VEE-mohs)	we lived
ellos/ellas/ustedes vivieron (vee-VYEHR-ohn)	they/you (plural) lived

The following are a few of the commonest irregular verbs in the simple past tense:

ser (to be)

yo fui (fooee)	I was
él/ella/usted fue (fooay)	he/she was/you were
nosotros/as fuimos (FOOEE-mohs)	we were
ellos/ellas/ustedes fueron (FOOYER-ohn)	they/you (plural) were

ir (to go)

The simple past of *ir* is exactly the same as the simple past of *ser*. Only context makes it clear which verb these forms represent.

estar (to be)

yo estuve   I was
(ess-TOO-vay)

él/ella/usted estuvo he/she was, you were
(ess-TOO-voh)

nosotros/as estuvimos we were
(ess-too-VEE-mohs)

ellos/ellas/ustedes   they/you (plural)
   estuvieron   were
(ess-too-VEEAYR-ohn)

tener (to have)

yo tuve   I had
(TOO-vay)

él/ella/usted tuvo he/she/you had
(TOO-voh)

nosotros/as tuvimos we had
(too-VEE-mohs)

21

ellos/ellas/ustedes   they/you had
    tuvieron
(too-VEEAY-rohn)

There are many other verb tenses in Spanish. However, a rudimentary knowledge of the above—simple present, the simple past and substitute for the future—will go a long way in helping the traveler to communicate basic information in Spanish.

Negatives

To make a sentence negative, simply put the word *no* directly before the verb.

"I buy fruit in that store."
Yo compro fruta en esa tienda.
(Yoh COHM-proh FROO-tah ayn ESS-ah tee-AYN-dah.)

"I don't buy fruit in that store."
Yo no compro fruta en esa tienda.
(Yoh no COHM-proh FROO-tah ayn ESS-ah tee-AYN-dah.)

Questions

There are several ways of forming questions in Spanish. The most usual way is to invert the subject and verb of the sentence.

"You sold the car."
Usted vendió el carro.
(Oo-STAY vayn-DEEOH el CAH-roh.)

"Did you sell the car?"
¿Vendió usted el carro?
(¿Vayn-DEEOH oo-STAY el CAH-roh?)

Note the inverted question mark at the beginning of the question.

Adverbs

In Spanish, many adverbs end with *mente*. This ending is like the "ly" in English. Thus the word *lentamente* (layn-tah-MAYN-tay) is equivalent to "slowly" in English. There are, however, many other adverbs in Spanish that do not end in *mente* and simply have to be learned as adverbs. For example, another word for "slowly" is *despacio* (days-PAH-see-oh).

Prepositions

These pesky little words tend to be the last forms to be mastered in any foreign language. This is because their use varies so much from one language to another.

For example, in English one speaks "to" someone; in Spanish one speaks "with" someone. In English you get married "to" someone; in Spanish, "with" someone. In English you "take care of"; in Spanish, the concept of "take care of" is contained in the verb *cuidar* and is not followed by a separate preposition.

Though problematic, prepositions will only occasionally lead to misunderstanding.

ABBREVIATIONS

Parts of Speech and Other Relevant Terms

adjective	adj.
adverb	adv.
article	art.
common usage	com.
conjunction	conj.
familiar	fam.
formal	for.
legal	leg.
medical	med.
noun	n.
plural	plu.
political	pol.
preposition	prep.
pronoun	pron.
singular	sing.
verb	v.

Countries and Regions

Andes	*Andes*
Argentina	*Arg.*
Bolivia	*Bol.*
Caribbean	*Carib.*
Central America	*CA*
Chile	*Chi.*
Colombia	*Col.*
Costa Rica	*CR*
Cuba	*Cuba*
Dominican Republic	*Dom.*
Ecuador	*Ec.*
El Salvador	*Sal.*
Guatemala	*Gua.*
Honduras	*Hon.*
Latin America	*LA*
Nicaragua	*Nic.*
Panama	*Pan.*
Paraguay	*Para.*
Peru	*Pe.*
Puerto Rico	*PR*
River Plate	*RP*
South America	*SA*
Uruguay	*Uru.*
Venezuela	*Ven.*

Spanish-English Dictionary

A

a (ah) prep. at; to

abajo (ah-BAH-hoh) adv. below; under; underneath

abarrotes (ah-bah-ROH-tays) n. *Mex.* groceries

abierto (ah-bee-AYR-toh) adj. open

abogado (ah-boh-GAH-doh) n. lawyer

abordo (ah-BORH-doh) on board

abrazo (ah-BRAH-soh) n. embrace

abrigo (ah-BREE-goh) n. coat

abril (ah-BREEL) n. April

abrir (ah-BREER) v. open

absolutamente (ahb-soh-loo-tah-MAYN-tay) adv. absolutely

abuela (ah-BWAY-lah) n. grandmother

abuelo (ah-BWAY-loh) n. grandfather

accidente (ahk-see-DAYN-tay) n. accident

acción (ahk-see-OHN) n. action; (com.) stock certificate

accionista (ahk-see-oh-NEES-tah) n. (com.)
     stockholder

aceite (ah-SAY-tay) n. oil

aceituna (ay-say-TOO-nah) n. olive

acelerar (ay-say-lay-RAHR) v. accelerate

acento (ah-SAYN-toh) n. accent

aceptar (ah-sayp-TAHR) v. accept

acera (ah-SAY-rah) n. sidewalk (except *Mex. RP*)

acerca de (ah-SAYR-cah day) prep. about

actividad (ahk-tee-vee-DAHD) n. activity

actor (ahk-TOHR) n. actor

actual (ahk-too-AHL) adj. present

acuerdo (ah-KUAYR-doh) n. agreement

adentro (ah-DAYN-troh) adv. within

adicional (ah-dee-see-oh-NAHL) adj. additional

adiós (ah-dee-OHS) interj. good-bye

admisión (ahd-mee-see-OHN) n. admission

admitir (ahd-mee-TEEHR) v. admit; allow

aduana (ah-DWAH-nah) n. customs

aeropuerto (ah-ay-roh-PWAYR-toh) n. airport

afeitar(se) (ah-fay-TAHR-say) v. shave

agencia (ah-HAYN-see-ah) n. agency; *Chi.* pawnshop

agente (ah-HAYN-tay) n. agent

agosto (ah-GOHS-toh) n. August

agua (AH-gwah) n. water

aguamala (ah-gwah-MAH-lah) n. *Carib., Mex.* jellyfish

agudo (ah-GOO-doh) adj. sharp

agujero (ah-goo-HAY-roh) n. hole (bored)

ahora (ah-OH-rah) adv. now

ahora mismo (ah-OH-rah MEES-moh) adv. right now

ahorrar (ah-oh-RAHR) v. save (money)

aire (AH-ee-ray) n. air

aire acondicionado (AH-ee-ray ah-cohn-dee-see-oh-NAH-doh) n. air conditioning

ají (ah-HEE) n. *Cuba, Ven.* bell pepper

ajo (AH-hoh) n. garlic

albaricoque (ahl-bah-ree-COH-kay) n. apricot (except *Arg., Mex., Uru.*)

alberca (ahl-BAYR-cah) n. *Mex.* swimming pool

alcohol (ahl-COHL) n. alcohol

alfombra (ahl-FOHM-brah) n. carpet

algo (AHL-goh) pron. something; adv. somewhat

algodón (ahl-goh-DOHN) n. cotton

alguien (AHL-ghee-ayn) pron. someone; anyone

alguno (ahl-GOO-noh) adj. some; any

algunos (ahl-GOO-nohs) pron. some

al lado de (ahl LAH-doh day) prep. beside

almacén (ahl-mah-SAYN) n. warehouse; store; *Arg.*
   food store; *Mex.* department store

al menos (ahl MAY-nohs) at least

almuerzo (ahl-moo-AYR-soh) n. lunch; midday meal
   (except *Mex.*)

al por mayor (ahl pohr mah-YOHR) adv. wholesale

alquilar (ahl-key-LAHR) v. rent

alto (AHL-toh) adj. tall; high

altura (ahl-TOO-rah) n. altitude; height

allí (ah-EE) adv. over there

allí mismo (ah-EE MEES-moh) adv. right there

amar (ah-MAHR) v. love

amarillo (ah-mah-REE-yoh) n., adj. yellow

ámbar (AHM-bahr) n. amber

ambulancia (ahm-boo-LAHN-see-ah) n. ambulance

a menos que (ah MAY-nohs kay) conj. unless

amigo(a) (ah-MEE-goh/gah) n. friend

amor (ah-MOHR) n. love

ananá (ah-nah-NAH) n. *Arg.* pineapple

ancho (AHN-choh) adj. broad; wide

ante (AHN-tay) prep. before

antes de que (AHN-tays day kay) conj. before

anteojos (ahn-tay-OH-hohs) n. *RP* eyeglasses

antigüedad (ahn-tee-gway-DAHD) n. antique

antiguo (ahn-TEE-gwoh) adj. ancient

anual (ah-noo-AHL) adj. annual

anunciar (ah-noon-see-AHR) v. announce; advertise

anuncio comercial (ah-NOON-see-oh coh-mayr-see-AHL) n. advertisement

año (AHN-yoh) n. year

apagar (ah-pah-GAHR) v. put out; turn off

apartamento (ah-pahr-tah-MAYN-toh) n. apartment (except *Mex.*)

aparte (ah-PAHR-tay) adv. apart

apellido (ah-pay-YEE-doh) n. last name

aprender (ah-prayn-DAYR) v. learn

aquí (ah-KEY) adv. here

archivar (ahr-chee-VAHR) v. file

archivo (ahr-CHEE-voh) n. archives; file

área (AH-ray-ah) n. area

aretes (ah-RAY-tays) n. *Cuba, Mex.* earrings

arma (AHR-mah) n. weapon

aros (AH-rohs) n. *Arg., Chi.* earrings

arreglar (ah-ray-GLAHR) v. arrange; fix

arroz (ah-ROHS) n. rice

arte (AHR-tay) n. art

artículo (ahr-TEE-coo-loh) n. article

artista (ahr-TEES-tah) n. artist; entertainer

asado (ah-SAH-doh) adj. roasted; n. *RP* steak;
   barbecue

ascensor (ah-sayn-SOHR) n. *Arg., Ecu., Pe., Uru., Ven.*
   elevator

asegurar (ah-say-goo-RAHR) v. secure; insure

asiento (ah-see-AYN-toh) n. seat

asistente (ah-sees-TAYN-tay) n. assistant

asistir (ah-sees-TEER) v. attend

aterrizaje (ah-tay-ree-SAH-hay) n. landing

a través de (ah trah-VAYS day) prep. through; across

aumentar (ah-oo-mayn-TAHR) v. increase

aún (ah-OON) adv. still; yet

aunque (ah-OON-kay) conj. although

auto (AH-oo-toh) n. car

autobus (AH-oo-toh-boos) n. *Ven.* city bus; *Arg., Chi.,*
   Cuba, Mex. intercity bus

automático (ah-oo-toh-MAH-tee-coh) adj. automatic

avance (ah-VAHN-say) n. advance payment

avanzar (ah-vahn-SAHR) v. advance

a veces (ah VAY-says) adv. sometimes

avenida (ah-vay-NEE-dah) n. avenue

avión (ah-vee-OHN) n. airplane

ayer (ah-YAYR) adv. yesterday

ayuda (ah-YOO-dah) n. help

32

ayudar (ah-yoo-DAHR) v. help

azúcar (ah-SOO-cahr) n. sugar

azulejo (ah-soo-LAY-hoh) n. glazed tile

B

bailar (bah-ee-LAHR) v. dance

bajar (bah-HAR) v. go down

banco (BAHN-coh) n. bench; bank

bandera (bahn-DAY-rah) n. flag

banqueta (bahn-KAY-tah) n. *Mex.* sidewalk

bañadera (bah-nyah-DAY-rah) n. *Arg., Cuba* bathtub

bañar (bah-NYAHR) v. bathe

bañar(se) (bah-NYAHR-say) v. take a bath

bañera (bah-NYAY-rah) n. *PR, Uru., Ven.* bathtub

baño (BAH-nyoh) n. bath; bathroom

bar (bahr) n. bar

barata (bah-RAH-tah) n. *Mex.* sale

barato (bah-RAH-toh) adj. cheap

barbero (bahr-BAY-roh) n. barber

barco (BAHR-coh) n. boat

base (BAH-say) n. base; basis; *Mex.* permanent; wave

bastante (bahs-TAHN-tay) adv. enough

basura (bah-SOO-rah) n. garbage

batería (bah-tay-REE-ah) n. battery (car)

baúl (bah-OOL) n. trunk

beber (bay-BAYR) v. drink

bebé (bay-BAY) n. baby

bebida (bay-BEE-dah) n. drink; beverage

bello (BAY-yoh) adj. beautiful; handsome

besar (bay-SAHR) v. kiss

beso (BAY-soh) n. kiss

betabel (bay-tah-BAYL) n. *Mex.* beet

biblioteca (beeb-lee-oh-TAY-cah) n. library

bicicleta (bee-cee-CLAY-tah) n. bicycle

bicho (BEE-choh) n. insect; small animal; *Cuba*
   shrewd operator; *PR* (vulgar)

bien (bee-AYN) adv. well; very

bien cocido (bee-AYN coh-SEE-doh) adj. well done
   (meat)

¡Bienvenido! (bee-ayn-vay-NEE-doh) interj. Welcome!

bife (BEE-fay) n. *RP* steak

biftec (beef-TAYK) n. beefsteak

billete (bee-YAY-tay) n. bill (money)

billetera (bee-yay-TAY-rah) n. *Bol., Chi., Cuba, Ec.,
   Pe.* wallet

bistec (bees-TAYK) n. *Cuba, Mex., Pe.* beefsteak

bizcocho (bees-COH-choh) n. *Cuba* ladyfinger; *PR*
   cake, *Mex.* (vulgar)

blanco (BLAHN-coh) n., adj. white

blanquillo (blahn-KEY-yoh) n. *Gua., Mex.* egg (euphemism for *huevo,* which has a double meaning)

blusa (BLOO-sah) n. blouse

boca (BOH-cah) n. mouth

bocaditos (boh-cah-DEE-tohs) n. *Cuba* little sandwiches; *Pe.* snacks

bodega (boh-DAY-gah) n. store; warehouse; *Cuba, Pe., PR, Ven.* grocery store

boga (BOH-gah) n. *Arg.* attorney

bolero (boh-LAY-roh) n. *Mex.* shoeshine boy

boleto (boh-LAY-toh) n. ticket

bolsa (BOHL-sah) n. bag; stock market; *Mex.* purse; *Ec., Pe., Uru.* shopping bag

bombilla (bohm-BEE-yah) n. light bulb (except *Mex.*)

bondadoso (bohn-dah-DOH-soh) adj. kind

bonito (boh-NEE-toh) adj. pretty

borrar (boh-RAHR) v. erase

botana (boh-TAH-nah) n. *Mex.* snack

botella (boh-TAY-yah) n. bottle

botica (boh-TEE-cah) n. *Carib.* drug store

botón (boh-TOHN) n. button

botones (boh-TOH-nays) n. bellboy

brazalete (brah-sah-LAY-tay) n. bracelet

brazo (BRAH-soh) n. arm

breve (BRAY-vay) adj. brief

broma (BROH-mah) n. joke

brujería (broo-hay-REE-ah) n. witchcraft

bueno (BWAY-noh) adj. good

bufete (boo-FAY-tay) n. *Mex.* law office

buscar (boos-CAHR) v. look for

C

caballero (cah-bah-YAY-roh) n. gentleman

caballo (cah-BAH-yoh) n. horse

cabello (cah-BAY-yoh) n. hair

cabeza (cah-BAY-sah) n. head

cacahuates (cah-cah-oo-AH-tays) n. *Mex.* peanuts

cada (CAH-dah) adj. each; every

cada uno (CAH-dah OO-noh) pron. every one

café (cah-FAY) n. coffee; café; n., adj. *Mex.* brown

caja (CAH-hah) n. box; safe; cashier's window

caja de seguridad (CAH-hah day say-goo-ree-DAHD)
    n. safe-deposit box

cajero (cah-HAY-roh) n. cashier; teller

cajón (cah-HON) n. drawer

calcetín (cahl-say-TEEN) n. sock

calefacción (cah-lah-fahk-see-OHN) n. central heating

calendario (cah-layn-DAH-ree-oh) n. calendar

calentura (cah-layn-TOO-rah) n. *Mex.* fever

calidad (cah-lee-DAHD) n. quality

caliente (cah-lee-AYN-tay) adj. hot

calor (cah-LOHR) n. heat

calle (CAH-yay) n. street

cama (CAH-mah) n. bed

cámara (CAH-mah-rah) n. camera; chamber

camarero (cah-mah-RAY-roh) n. waiter

camarón (cah-mah-ROHN) n. shrimp

cambiar (cahm-bee-AHR) v. change; exchange

cambio (CAHM-bee-oh) n. change; exchange

cambur (cahm-BOOR) n. *Ven.* banana

caminar (cah-mee-NAHR) v. walk

camino (cah-MEE-noh) n. road

camión (cah-mee-OHN) n. truck; *Mex.* city bus

camisa (cah-MEE-sah) n. shirt

campamento (cahm-pah-MAYN-toh) n. camp

campo (CAHM-poh) n. country (rural area)

canasta (cah-NAHS-tah) n. basket

canción (cahn-see-OHN) n. song

canela (cah-NAY-lah) n. cinnamon

cansado (cahn-SAH-doh) adj. tired

cantante (cahn-TAHN-tay) n. singer

cantar (cahn-TAHR) v. sing

cantidad (cahn-tee-DAHD) n. amount

cañón (cah-NYOHN) n. canyon

capital (cah-pee-TAHL) n. capital

cara (CAH-rah) n. face

carburador (cahr-boo-rah-DOHR) n. carburetor

cárcel (CAHR-sayl) n. jail

carga (CAHR-gah) n. freight; cargo

cargamento (cahr-gah-MAYN-toh) n. load; shipment

carne (CAHR-nay) n. meat

carne de puerco (CAHR-nay day PWAYR-coh) n. pork

carne de res (CAHR-nay day rays) n. beef

carnet de manejar (cahr-NAYT day mah-nay-HAHR)
    n. *Chi.* driver's license

caro (CAH-roh) adj. expensive

carreta (cah-RAY-tah) n. cart

carretera (cah-ray-TAY-rah) n. highway

carro (CAH-roh) n. car

carta (CAHR-tah) n. letter

casa (CAH-sah) n. house; home

casaca (cah-SAH-cah) n. *Pe.* jacket

casa de correos (CAH-sayh day coh-RAY-ohs) n. post
    office (except *Mex.*)

casado (cah-SAH-doh) adj. married

casi (CAH-see) adv. almost

caso (CAH-soh) n. case

catedral (cah-tay-DRAHL) n. cathedral

causa (CAH-oo-sah) n. cause; lawsuit

causar (cah-oo-SAHR) v. cause

cazar (cah-SAHR) v. hunt

cebolla (say-BOH-yah) n. onion

cédula de identidad (SAY-doo-lah day ee-dayn-tee-DAHD) n. *Bol., Ec., Mex., Pe., RP* ID card

centavo (sayn-TAH-voh) n. cent

central (sayn-TRAHL) adj. central

cepillo de dientes (say-PEE-yoh day dee-AYN-tays) n. toothbrush

cerámica (say-RAH-mee-cah) n. ceramics

cerca (SAYR-cah) adv. near

cerillo (say-REE-yoh) n. *CA, Mex.* match

cero (SAY-roh) n. zero

cerrar (say-RAHR) v. close

certificado (sayr-tee-fee-CAH-doh) n. certificate

cerveza (sayr-VAY-sah) n. beer

chabacano (chah-bah-CAH-noh) n. *Mex.* apricot

chamaco (chah-MAH-coh) n. *Mex.* boy; kid

chamarra (chah-MAH-rah) n. *Mex.* jacket

champaña (chahm-PAH-nyah) n. champagne

champú (chahm-POO) n. shampoo

chaqueta (chah-KAY-tah) n. jacket

chauchas (CHAH-oo-chahs) n. *RP* green beans

cheque (CHAY-kay) n. check

chicle (CHEE-clay) n. chewing gum

chico (CHEE-coh) n. kid; adj. small

chile (CHEE-lay) n. chilli pepper

chiste (CHEE-stay) n. joke

chocar (choh-CAHR) v. collide

chocolate (choh-coh-LAH-tay) n. chocolate

chofer (choh-FAYR) n. driver

chorizo (choh-REE-soh) n. salami-type sausage

chuleta (choo-LAY-tah) n. chop; cutlet

cielo (see-AY-loh) n. sky; heaven

cien (see-AYN) n., adj. one hundred

ciento (see-AYN-toh) n., adj. one hundred

cierre (see-AY-ray) n. *Mex. Uru.* zipper

cigarrillo (see-gah-REE-yoh) n. *Ec., Pan., Pe., RP* cigarette

cigarro (see-GAH-roh) n. cigarette; *Ec., PR,* cigar

cinco (SEEN-coh) n., adj. five

cincuenta (seen-KWAYN-tah) n., adj. fifty

cinturón (seen-too-ROHN) n. belt

círculo (SEER-coo-loh) n. circle

cita (SEE-tah) n. appointment; date

ciudad (see-oo-DAHD) n. city

ciudadano (see-oo-da-DAH-noh) n. citizen

clase (KLAH-say) n. class; kind

cliente (clee-AYN-tay) n. customer; client

clima (KLEE-mah) n. climate; *Mex.* air conditioning

cobija (coh-BEE-hah) n. *Mex.* blanket

cocina (coh-SEE-nah) n. kitchen; stove

cocinar (coh-see-NAHR) v. cook

coche (COH-chay) n. car

cochera (coh-CHAY-rah) n. *Mex.* garage

colectivo (coh-layk-TEE-voh) n. *Arg., Bol.* city bus;
     adj. collective

colgador (cohl-gah-DOHR) n. clothes hanger

color (coh-LOHR) n. color

comedor (coh-may-DORH) n. dining room

comenzar (coh-mayn-SAHR) v. begin

comer (coh-MAYR) v. eat

comercial (coh-mayr-see-AHL) adj. commercial

cómico (COH-mee-coh) n. comedian; adj. funny

comercio (coh-MAYR-see-oh) n. business

comida (coh-MEE-dah) n. food; meal

comisión (coh-mee-see-OHN) n. commission

como (COH-moh) adv. as; like; conj. as; when; if; so that

¿cómo? (COH-moh) adv. how?

cómodo (COH-moh-doh) adj. comfortable

compañero (cohm-pah-NYAY-roh) n. companion; partner

compañía (cohm-pah-NYEE-ah) n. company

compartir (cohm-pahr-TEER) v. share

compinche (cohm-PEEN-chay) n. *Bol., RP* buddy

completo (cohm-PLAY-toh) adj. complete

comprador (cohm-prah-DOHR) n. buyer

comprar (cohm-PRAHR) v. buy

comprender (cohm-prayn-DAYR) v. understand

computadora (cohm-poo-tah-DOH-rah) n. computer

con (cohn) prep. with

concierto (cohn-see-AYR-toh) n. concert

conclusión (cohn-cloo-see-OHN) n. conclusion

condición (cohn-dee-see-OHN) n. condition

conducir (cohn-doo-SEER) v. drive

conferencia (cohn-fay-RAYN-see-ah) n. lecture

confiar (cohn-fee-AHR) v. trust

congreso (cohn-GRAY-soh) n. congress; convention

conocer (coh-noh-SAYR) v. know; be acquainted with

conocimiento (coh-noh-see-mee-AYN-toh) n. knowledge

consejo (cohn-SAY-hoh) n. advice

considerado (cohn-see-day-RAH-doh) adj. considerate

consignación (cohn-seeg-nah-see-OHN) n.
consignment

constituir (cohn-stee-too-EER) v. constitute

construcción (cohn-strook-see-OHN) n. construction

consulado (cohn-soo-LAH-doh) n. consulate

consultar (cohn-sool-TAHR) v. consult

consultorio (cohn-sool-TOH-ree-oh) n. doctor's office

contacto (cohn-TAHK-toh) n. contact; *Mex.* (elec.)
outlet

contador (cohn-tah-DOHR) n. accountant

contar (cohn-TAHR) v. count

contener (cohn-tay-NAYR) v. contain

contenido (cohn-tay-NEE-doh) n. content

contestar (cohn-tays-TAHR) v. answer

continuar (cohn-tee-noo-AHR) v. continue

contra (COHN-trah) prep. against

contrato (cohn-TRAH-toh) n. contract

contribuir (cohn-tree-boo-EER) v. contribute

conveniente (cohn-vay-nee-AYN-tay) adj. convenient

conversar (cohn-vayr-SAHR) v. converse

coñac (coh-NYAK) n. cognac; brandy

copa (COH-pah) n. wineglass; *Mex.* drink (alcoholic)

copiar (coh-pee-AHR) v. copy

corazón (coh-rah-SOHN) n. heart

corbata (cohr-BAH-tah) n. necktie

corporación (cohr-poh-rah-see-OHN) n. corporation

correcto (coh-RAYK-toh) adj. correct

corredor (coh-ray-DOHR) n. runner; corridor

corredor de bolsa (coh-ray-DOHR day BOHL-sah) n.
    stockbrocker

correo (coh-RAY-oh) n. mail; post office

correr (coh-RAYR) v. run

cortar (cohr-TAHR) v. cut

cortina (cohr-TEE-nah) n. curtain

corto (COHR-toh) adj. short

cosa (COH-sah) n. thing

crédito (CRAY-dee-toh) n. credit

creer (cray-AYR) v. believe

criada (cree-AH-dah) n. maid

criado (cree-AH-doh) n. servant

crimen (CREE-mayn) n. crime

cuadra (KWAH-drah) n. city block

cuadro (KWAH-droh) n. square; picture

cualquiera (kwal-key-AY-rah) pron. whichever;
    whoever

cualquier cosa (kwayl-key-AYR COH-sah) pron.
    anything

cuando (KWAN-doh) adv. when

¿cuántos? (KWAN-tohs) adj., pron. how many?

cuarenta (kwah-RAYN-tah) n., adj. forty

cuarto (KWAHR-toh) adj. fourth; n. quarter; room

cuarto de dormir (KWAHR-toh day dohr-MEER) n. bedroom

cuate (KWAH-tay) n. *Mex.* twin; buddy

cuatro (KWAH-troh) n., adj. four

cubrir (coo-BREER) v. cover

cuchara (coo-CHAH-rah) n. spoon

cuchillito de afeitar (coo-chee-YEE-toh day ah-fay-TAHR) n. *Cuba* razor blade

cuchillo (coo-CHEE-yoh) n. knife

cuello (coo-AY-yoh) n. neck; collar

cuenta (coo-AYN-tah) n. account; bill

cuero (coo-AY-roh) n. leather

cuerpo (coo-AYR-poh) n. body

cueva (coo-AY-vah) n. cave

¡Cuidado! (coo-ee-DAH-doh) imper. Be careful!

cuidar (coo-ee-DAHR) v. take care of

cultura (cool-TOO-rah) n. culture

cumpleaños (coom-play-AH-nyohs) n. birthday

cuneta (coo-NAY-tah) n. *Chi.* sidewalk

cura (COO-rah) n. cure; priest

curar (coo-RAHR) v. treat; cure

D

dañar (dah-NYAHR) v. hurt

daño (DAH-nyoh) n. damage

dar (dahr) v. give

dar(se) cuenta de (DAHR-say coo-AYN-tah day) v. realize

dar(se) prisa (DAHR-say PREE-sah) v. hurry

de (day) prep. of; from; about

deber (day-BAYR) n. duty; v. owe; ought to; must; should

débil (DAY-beel) adj. weak

decir (day-SEER) v. say; tell

decisión (day-see-see-OHN) n. decision

declaración (day-clah-rah-see-OHN) n. declaration; statement

declarar (de-clah-RAHR) v. declare

dedo (DAY-doh) n. finger

dedo del pie (DAY-doh del pee-AY) n. toe

delgado (dayl-GAH-doh) adj. thin

delicioso (day-lee-see-OH-soh) adj. delicious

demanda (day-MAHN-dah) n. demand; lawsuit

demandar (day-mahn-DAHR) v. demand; sue

demasiado (day-mah-see-AH-doh) adj; pron. too much

demostrar (day-moh-STRAHR) v. demonstrate

dentista (dayn-TEE-stah) n. dentist

departamento (day-pahr-tah-MAYN-toh) n. department; *Mex.* apartment

dependiente (day-payn-dee-AYN-tay) n. clerk; adj. dependent

deporte (day-POHR-tay) n. sport

depositar (day-poh-see-TAHR) v. deposit

deposito (day-POH-see-toh) n. deposit

derecho (day-RAY-choh) n. right; law; adj. right; straight; adv. straight ahead

de repente (day ray-PAYN-tay) adv. suddenly

desagradable (day-sah-grah-DAH-blay) adj. disagreeable

desayuno (day-sah-YOO-noh) n. breakfast

descansar (days-cahn-SAHR) v. rest

describir (days-cree-VEER) v. discover

descripción (days-creep-see-OHN) n. description

descubrir (days-coo-VREER) v. describe

descuento (days-coo-AYN-toh) n. discount

desde (DAYS-day) prep. from; since

desear (day-say-AHR) v. desire; want

desocupado (day-soh-coo-PAH-doh) adj. unoccupied

despacio (days-PAH-see-oh) adv. slowly

despertador (days-payr-tah-DOHR) n. alarm clock

después (days-poo-AYS) adv. after; afterwards

detalle (day-TAH-yay) n. detail

detener (day-tay-NAYR) v. stop

determinar (day-tayr-mee-NAHR) v. determine

detrás (day-TRAHS) adv. behind

deuda (DAY-oo-dah) n. debt

de vez en cuando (day vays ayn KWAN-doh) adv. once in a while

devolver (day-vohl-VAYR) v. return; give back

día (DEE-ah) n. day

día festivo (DEE-ah fay-STEE-voh) n. holiday

día laborable (DEE-ah lah-boh-RAH-blay) n. workday

diamante (dee-ah-MAHN-tay) n. diamond

diario (dee-AH-ree-oh) n. daily paper; adj. daily

diciembre (dee-see-AYM-bray) n. December

diente (dee-AYN-tay) n. tooth

diez (dee-AYS) n., adj. ten

diez y nueve (dee-AYS ee noo-AY-vay) n., adj. nineteen

diez y ocho (dee-AYS ee OH-choh) n., adj. eighteen

diferencia (dee-fay-RAYN-see-ah) n. difference

diferente (dee-fay-RAYN-tay) adj. different

difícil (dee-FEE-seel) adj. difficult

dinero (dee-NAY-roh) n. money

dios (dee-OHS) n. god

dirección (dee-rayk-see-OHN) n. direction; address

directo (dee-RAYK-toh) adj. direct

director (dee-rayk-TOHR) n. director; manager

dirigente (dee-ree-HAYN-tay) n. leader

dirigir (dee-ree-HEER) v. direct; manage

discurso (dees-COOR-soh) n. speech

discutir (dees-coo-TEER) v. argue

disponible (dees-poh-NEE-blay) adj. available

distancia (dees-TAHN-see-ah) n. distance

distante (dees-TAHN-tay) adj. distant

distribuir (dees-tree-boo-EER) v. distribute

diversión (dee-vayr-see-OHN) n. recreation

divertido (dee-vayr-TEE-doh) adj. amusing

divertir (dee-vayr-TEER) v. amuse

divertir(se) (dee-vayr-TEER-say) v. have a good time

división (dee-vee-see-OHN) n. division

doble (DOH-blay) adj. double

doce (DOH-say) n., adj. twelve

docena (doh-SAY-nah) n. dozen

doctor (dohk-TOHR) n. doctor

dólar (DOH-lahr) n. dollar

dolor (doh-LOHR) n. pain

dolor de cabeza (doh-LOHR day cah-BAY-sah) n.
   headache

dolor de estómago (doh-LOHR day ays-TOH-mah-goh) n. stomachache

dolor de muela (doh-LOHR day moo-AY-lah) n. toothache

domingo (doh-MEEN-goh) n. Sunday

¿dónde? (DOHN-day) adv. where?

dormir (dohr-MEER) v. sleep

dormitorio (dohr-mee-TOHR-ee-oh) n. *Bol., Ec., Pe.* bedroom

dos (dohs) n., adj. two

dos veces (dohs VAY-says) adv. twice

drama (DRAH-mah) n. drama; play

droga (DROH-gah) n. drug

ducha (DOO-chah) n. *Cuba, Pe., PR* shower

dueño (doo-AY-nyoh) n. owner

dulce (DOOL-say) adj. sweet; *Pan.* cake

dulces (DOOL-says) n. candy

durante (doo-RAHN-tay) prep. during

durazno (doo-RAHS-noh) n. *Arg., CA, Mex., Pan., Pe.* peach

duro (DOO-roh) adj. hard

E

economía (ay-coh-noh-MEE-ah) n. economy

echar al correo (ay-CHAHR ahl coh RAY oh) v. mail

edad (ay-DAHD) n. age

efectivo (ay-fayk-TEE-voh) n. cash; adj. effective

eficiente (ay-fee-see-AYN-tay) adj. efficient

ejemplo (ay-HAYM-ploh) n. example

ejotes (ay-HOH-tays) n. *Mex.* green beans

el (ayl) masc. art. the

él (ayl) pron. he

elemento (ay-lay-MAYN-toh) n. element

elevador (ay-lay-vah-DOHR) n. *Carib., Mex.* elevator

ella (AY-yah) pron. she

ellos (AY-yohs) pron. they

embajada (aym-bah-HAH-dah) n. embassy

embajador (aym-bah-hah-DOHR) n. ambassador

emparedado (aym-pah-ray-DAH-doh) n. *Bol.*
  sandwich

empate (aym-PAH-tay) n. *Ven.* girlfriend

empezar (aym-pay-SAHR) v. begin

empleada (aym-lay-AH-dah) n. *Bol., Ec., Uru., Pan.*
  maid

emplear (aym-play-AHR) v. employ; use

empleo (aym-PLAY-oh) n. job

empresa (aym-PRAY-sah) n. company

empujar (aym-poo-HAHR) v. push

en (ayn) prep. in; on

encaje (ayn-CAH-hay) n. lace

en casa (ayn CAH-sah) adv. at home

encender (ayn-sayn-DAYR) v. light

encontrar (ayn-cohn-TRAHR) v. find; meet

en el extranjero (ayn ayl ays-trahn-HAY-roh) adv.
    abroad

enero (ay-NAY-roh) n. January

enfermo (ayn-FAYR-moh) adj. sick

engañar (ayn-gahn-YAHR) v. deceive; cheat

ensalada (ayn-sah-LAH-dah) n. salad

en seguida (ayn say-GHEE-dah) adv. at once

enseñar (ayn-say-NYAHR) v. teach

entendimiento (ayn-tayn-dee-mee-AYN-toh) n.
    understanding

entero (ayn-TAY-roh) adj. entire

en todas partes (ayn TOH-dahs PAHR-tays) adv.
    everywhere

entonces (ayn-TOHN-says) adv. then

entrada (ayn-TRAH-dah) n. entrance; *Bol.* ticket

entrar (ayn-TRAHR) v. enter; come in

entre (AYN-tray) prep. between; among

entregar (ayn-tray-GAHR) v. deliver

entremeses (ayn-tray-MAY-says) n. hors d'oeuvres

envase (ayn-VAH-say) n. container

en vez de (ayn vays day) prep. instead of

enviar (ayn-vee-AHR) v. send

equipaje (ay-key-PAH-hay) n. luggage

equipo (ay-KEY-poh) n. equipment; team

equivalente (ay-key-vah-LAYN-tay) n., adj. equivalent

equivocado (ay-key-voh-CAH-doh) adj. wrong; mistaken

equivocar(se) (ay-key-voh-CAHR-say) v. make a mistake

error (ay-ROHR) n. mistake

escalera (ays-cah-LAY-rah) n. stairs

escoger (ays-coh-HAYR) v. choose

esconder (ays-cohn-DAYR) v. hide

escribir (ays-cree-VEER) v. write

escritor (ays-cree-TOHR) n. writer

escuchar (ays-coo-CHAHR) v. listen to

escuela (ays-KWAY-lah) n. school

escultor (ays-cool-TOHR) n. sculptor

esmeralda (ays-may-RAHL-dah) n. emerald

estancia (ays-TAHN-see-ah) n. *RP* farm

¡Eso es! (AY-soh ays) interj. That's it!

especial (ays-pay-see-AHL) adj. special

espejuelos (ays-pay-HWAY-lohs) n. *Cuba* eyeglasses

esperar (ays-pay-RAHR) v. wait for; hope for; expect

espinacas (ays-pee-NAH-cahs) n. spinach

esposa (ays-POH-sah) n. wife

esposo (ays-POH-soh) n. husband

esquina (ays-KEY-nah) n. corner

establecer (ays-tah-blay-SAYR) v. establish

estación (ays-tah-see-OHN) n. station; season

estacionamiento (ays-tah-see-oh-nah-mee-AYN-toh)
   n. *Mex., Uru.* parking lot

estado de cuentas (ays-TAH-doh day coo-AYN-tahs)
   n. (com.) statement

estampilla (ays-tahm-PEE-yah) n. *Bol., Ec., Mex., PR*
   postage stamp

esta noche (AYS-tah NOH-chay) adv. tonight

estar (ays-TAHR) v. be

estatua (ays-TAH-too-ah) n. statue

este (AYS-tay) n. east; adj. this

estómago (ays-TOH-mah-goh) n. stomach

estudiante (ays-too-dee-AHN-tay) n. student

estudiar (ays-too-dee-AHR) v. study

etiqueta (ay-tee-KAY-tah) n. tag; label

evidente (ay-vee-DAYN-tay) adj. evident

evitar (ay-vee-TAHR) v. avoid

examen (ex-AH-mayn) n. examination

examinar (ex-ah-mee-NAHR) v. examine

exceso (ex-SAY-soh) n. excess

exclusivo (ex-kloo-SEE-voh) adj. exclusive

excursión (ex-coor-see-OHN) n. excursion

exhibición (ex-ee-bee-see-OHN) n. exhibit

éxito (EX-ee-toh) n. success

explicación (ex-plee-cah-see-OHN) n. explanation

explicar (ex-plee-CAHR) v. explain

exportación (ex-pohr-tah-see-OHN) n. export

exportar (ex-pohr-TAHR) v. export

exterior (ex-tay-ree-OHR) adj. exterior; foreign

extranjero (ex-trahn-HAY-roh) n. foreigner; adj.
   foreign

F

fácil (FAH-seel) adj. easy

fácilmente (FAH-seel-mayn-tay) adv. easily

falda (FAHL-dah) n. skirt; *Cuba* cut of beef

falta (FAHL-tah) n. lack

faltar (fahl-TAHR) v. lack; be absent

familia (fah-MEE-lee-ah) n. family

famoso (fah-MOH-soh) adj. famous

fantástico (fahn-TAHS-tee-coh) adj. fantastic

farmacia (fahr-MAH-see-ah) n. drugstore

febrero (fay-BRAY-roh) n. February

fecha (FAY-chah) n. date

felicitaciones (fay-lee-see-tah-see-OH-nays) n. congratulations

feliz (fay-LEES) adj. happy

feo (FAY-oh) adj. ugly; adv. *Arg., Col., Mex.* bad

ferretería (fay-ray-tay-REE-ah) n. hardware store

ferrocarril (fay-roh-cah-REEL) n. railroad

fiebre (fee-AY-bray) n. fever

fiesta (fee-AY-stah) n. party

finanza (fee-NAHN-sah) n. finance

finca (FEEN-cah) n. *Cuba* farm

fin de semana (feen day say-MAH-nah) n. weekend

fino (FEE-noh) adj. fine; refined

firma (FEER-mah) n. signature

firmar (feer-MAHR) v. sign

flojo (FLOH-hoh) adj. loose; *Mex., Ven.* lazy

foco (FOH-coh) n. focus; *Mex.* light bulb

fondo (FOHN-doh) n. bottom; rear

forma (FOHR-mah) n. form; shape

formar (fohr-MAHR) v. form; shape

fósforo (FOHS-foh-roh) n. match

foto (FOH-toh) n. photo

fracasar (frah-cah-SAHR) v. fail

fracaso (frah-CAH-soh) n. failure

frazada (frah-SAH-dah) n. blanket

frecuentemente (fray-kwayn-tay-MAYN-tay) adv.
    frequently

fresa (FRAY-sah) n. strawberry

fresco (FRAYS-coh) adj. fresh; cool

frijoles (free-HOH-lays) n. *Carib., Mex.* dry beans

frío (FREE-oh) n., adj. cold

frontera (frohn-TAY-rah) n. border

fruta (FROO-tah) n. fruit

fuera (FWAY-rah) adv. out; outside

fuerte (FWAYR-tay) adj. strong; loud

fumar (foo-MAHR) v. smoke

función (foon-see-OHN) n. function; performance

fusil (foo-SEEL) n. gun; rifle

fútbol (FOOT-bohl) n. soccer

fútbol americano (FOOT-bohl ah-may-ree-CAH-noh)
    n. football

G

galón (gah-LOHN) n. gallon

galleta (gah-YAY-tah) n. cracker; *Mex.* (also cookie)

ganancias (gah-NAHN-see-ahs) n. profit; *Gua., Mex.*
    bonus

ganar (gah-NAHR) v. win; earn

gancho (GAHN-choh) n. hook; *Mex.* hanger

ganga (GAHN-gah) n. bargain

garaje (gah-RAH-hay) n. garage

garantía (gah-rahn-TEE-ah) n. guaranty; warranty

garantizar (gah-rahn-tee-SAHR) v. guarantee

garganta (gahr-GAHN-tah) n. throat

gaseosa (gah-say-OH-sah) n. carbonated soft drink

gasolina (gah-soh-LEE-nah) n. gasoline

gastar (gah-STAHR) v. spend

gasto (GAH-stoh) n. expense

gato (GAH-toh) n. cat

general (hay-nay-RAHL) n. adj. general

gente (HAYN-tay) n. people

genuino (hay-noo-EE-noh) adj. genuine

gerencia (hay-RAYN-see-ah) n. management

gerente (hay-RAYN-tay) n. manager

gimnasio (heem-NAH-see-oh) n. gym

ginebra (hee-NAY-brah) n. gin

giro (HEE-roh) n. money order

gobernador (goh-bayr-nah-DOHR) n. governor

gobierno (goh-bee-AYR-noh) n. government

golf (golf) n. golf

golfo (GOHL-foh) n. gulf

goma (GOH-mah) n. rubber; *Cuba* tire; eraser; *Cuba, Ec., Uru.* glue

gordo (GOHR-doh) adj. fat; n. *Mex.* (term of affection)

gracias (GRAH-see-ahs) n. thanks

gran (grahn) adj. large; great

grande (GRAHN-day) adj. large; great

granja (GRAHN-hah) n. farm

gratis (GRAH-tees) adv. free (at no cost)

gripa (GREE-pah) n. *Mex.* flu

gripe (GREE-pay) n. flu

gris (grees) adj. gray

gritar (gree-TAHR) v. shout

grupo (GROO-poh) n. group

guagua (GWAH-gwah) n. *Chi.* baby; *Cuba* bus

guajiro (gwah-HEE-roh) n. *Cuba* peasant

guante (GWAHN-tay) n. glove

guapo (GWAH-poh) adj. handsome

güero (GWAY-roh) n. *Mex.* blond; fair complexion

guía (GHEE-ah) n. guide

guía telefónica (GHEE-ah tay-lay-FOH-nee-cah) n.
    Cuba, Ec., Pe., RP, Ven. telephone directory

guineo (ghee-NAY-oh) n. *Pan., PR* small banana

guisado (ghee-SAH-doh) n. stew

guiso (GHEE-soh) n. dish; *PR* stew

guitarra (ghee-TAH-rah) n. guitar

gustar (goo-STAHR) v. like

H

haber (ah-BAYR) v. have (auxiliary)

habichuelas (ah-bee-CHWAY-lahs) n. *Mex., Pan.* green beans

habitación (ah-bee-tah-see-OHN) n. room

hablar (ah-BLAHR) v. speak

hace (AH-say) adv. ago (ex. **hace un año**, a year ago)

hacer (ah-SAYR) v. do; make

hacia (AH-see-ah) prep. toward

hambre (AHM-bray) n. hunger

hamburguesa (ahm-boor-GAY-sah) n. hamburger

hasta (AH-stah) prep. until

hay (AH-ee) v. there is; there are

helado (ay-LAH-doh) n. ice cream

hermana (ayr-MAH-nah) n. sister

hermano (ayr-MAH-noh) n. brother

hermoso (ayr-MOH-soh) adj. beautiful

hielo (ee-AY-loh) n. ice

hija (EE-hah) n. daughter

hijo (EE-hoh) n. son

hoja (OH-hah) n. leaf; sheet (of paper)

hoja de afeitar (OH-hah day ah-fay-TAHR) n. razor blade

hoja de rasurar (OH-hah day rah-soo-RAHR) n. *Mex.* razor blade

hombre (OHM-bray) n. man

hombre de negocios (OHM-bray day nay-GOH-see-
   ohs) n. businessman

honesto (oh-NAYS-toh) adj. honest

hora (OH-rah) n. hour; time

horario (oh-RAH-ree-oh) n. schedule

horrible (oh-REE-blay) adj. horrible

hospital (ohs-pee-TAHL) n. hospital

hotel (oh-TAYL) n. hotel

hoy (oy) n., adv. today

hueco (WAY-coh) n. hole

huésped (WAYS-payd) n. guest

huevo (WAY-voh) n. egg

I

idea (ee-DAY-ah) n. idea

idioma (ee-dee-OH-mah) n. language

iglesia (ee-GLAY-see-ah) n. church

ilegal (ee-lay-GAHL) adj. illegal

imagen (ee-MAH-hen) n. image

imaginar (ee-mah-hee-NAHR) v. imagine

imperdible (eem-payr-DEE-blay) n. *Ec.* bobby pin

impermeable (eem-payr-may-AH-blay) n. raincoat

importaciones (eem-pohr-tah-see-OH-nays) n. imports

importador (eem-pohr-tah-DOHR) n. importer

importancia (eem-pohr-TAHN-see-ah) n. importance

importante (eem-pohr-TAHN-tay) adj. important

importar (eem-pohr-TAHR) v. import; matter

imposible (eem-poh-SEE-blay) adj. impossible

impresión (eem-pray-see-OHN) n. impression;
    printing

impresionante (eem-pray-see-oh-NAHN-tay) adj.
    impressive

impresionar (eem-pray-see-oh-NAHR) v. make an
    impression

impresor (eem-pray-SOHR) n. printer

impuesto (eem-PWAYS-toh) n. tax

impuesto de utilidades (eem-PWAYS-toh day oo-tee-
    lee-DAH-days) n. income tax

incluir (een-cloo-EER) v. include

incluso (een-CLOO-soh) adv. even

independiente (een-day-payn-dee-AYN-tay) adj.
    independent

indicar (een-dee-CAHR) v. indicate

industria (een-DOO-stree-ah) n. industry

inferior (een-fay-ree-OHR) adj. inferior; lower

informar (een-fohr-MAHR) v. inform

informe (een-FOHR-may) n. report

ingresos (een-GRAY-sohs) n. income

inmediatamente (een-may-dee-ah-tah-MAYN-tay) adv. immediately

inmigrante (een-mee-GRAHN-tay) n. immigrant

inodoro (een-oh-DOH-roh) n. toilet

insecto (een-SAYK-toh) n. insect

insistir (een-see-STEER) v. insist

inspeccionar (een-spayk-see-oh-NAHR) v. inspect

instituto (een-stee-TOO-toh) n. institute

instrucción (een-strook-see-OHN) n. instruction

insultar (een-sool-TAHR) v. insult

inteligente (een-tay-lee-HAYN-tay) adj. intelligent

intentar (een-tayn-TAHR) v. try; attempt

intérprete (een-TAYR-pray-tay) n. interpreter

invierno (een-vee-AYR-noh) n. winter; *SA* rainy season

invitación (een-vee-tah-see-OHN) n. invitation

invitado (een-vee-TAH-doh) n. guest

invitar (een-vee-TAHR) v. invite

ir (eer) v. go

ir de compras (eer day COHM-prahs) v. go shopping

ir de prisa (eer day PREE-sah) v. hurry

ir (se) (EER-say) v. go away

isla (EES-lah) n. island
izquierdo (ees-key-AYR-doh) adj. left

J

jabón (hah-BOHN) n. soap
jalar (hah-LAHR) v. pull
jamón (hah-MOHN) n. ham
jardín (hahr-DEEN) n. garden
jefe (HAY-fay) n. chief; boss
jíbaro (HEE-bah-roh) n. *PR* peasant
jitomate (hee-toh-MAH-tay) n. *Mex.* tomato
joven (HOH-vayn) n. young person; adj. young
joyería (hoh-yay-REE-ah) n. jewelry store
jueves (HWAY-vays) n. Thursday
jugar (hoo-GAHR) v. play; gamble
jugo de naranja (HOO-goh day nah-RAHN-hah) n.
    orange juice
julio (HOO-lee-oh) n. July
junio (HOON-nee-oh) n. June
justicia (hoos-TEE-see-ah) n. justice

K

kilo(gramo) (key-loh-GRAH-moh) n. kilogram
kilómetro (key-LOH-may-troh) n. kilometer (approx.
    ⅝ mile)

L

la (lah) fem. art. the

ladrón (lah-DROHN) n. thief

lago (LAH-goh) n. lake

lámpara (LAHM-pah-rah) n. lamp

lana (LAH-nah) n. wool; *Mex.* money (slang)

langosta (lahn-GOH-stah) n. lobster

lápiz (LAH-pees) n. pencil

largo (LAHR-goh) adj. long

las (lahs) f. plu. art. the

las onces (lahs OHN-says) n. *Chi.* snack

lata (LAH-tah) n. can

lavandería (lah-vahn-day-REE-ah) n. laundry

lavar (lah-VAHR) v. wash

leche (LAY-chay) n. milk

lechuga (lay-CHOO-gah) n. lettuce

leer (lay-AYR) v. read

lejos (LAY-hohs) adv. far

lente (LAYN-tay) n. lens

lentes (LAYN-tays) n. *Mex.* eyeglasses

levantar (lay-vahn-TAHR) v. raise; lift

ley (lay) n. law

libertad (lee-bayr-TAHD) n. freedom

libra (LEE-brah) n. pound

libre (LEE-bray) adj. free

libro (LEE-broh) n. book

licencia (lee-SAYN-see-ah) n. license

licenciado (lee-sayn-see-AH-doh) n. *Mex.* lawyer

licor (lee-COHR) n. liquor; liqueur

limón (lee-MOHN) n. lemon; lime

limonada (lee-moh-NAH-dah) n. lemonade

limosnero (lee-mohs-NAY-roh) n. beggar

limpiabotas (leem-pee-ah-BOH-tahs) n. *Carib., Ven.*
    shoeshine boy

limpio (LEEM-pee-oh) adj. clean

lindo (LEEN-doh) adj. pretty

lista (LEE-stah) n. list

listo (LEE-stoh) adj. ready; clever

llamar (yah-MAHR) v. call

llamar por teléfono (yah-MAHR pohr tay-LAY-foh-
    noh) v. phone

llanta (YAHN-tah) n. *Mex., Uru.* tire

llave (YAH-vay) n. key; *Mex., Pe.* faucet

llegada (yay-GAH-dah) n. arrival

llegar (yay-GAHR) v. arrive

lleno (YAY-noh) adj. full

llevar (yay-VAHR) v. take

llover (yoh-VAYR) v. rain

lluvia (YOO-vee-ah) n. rain

loco (LOH-coh) adj. crazy

los (lohs) m. plu. art. the

lotería (loh-tay-REE-ah) n. lottery

lucha (LOO-chah) n. struggle

lugar (loo-GAHR) n. place

lujo (LOO-hoh) n. luxury

luna de miel (LOO-nah day mee-AYL) n. honeymoon

luz (loos) n. light

M

madera (mah-DAY-rah) n. wood

madre (MAH-dray) n. mother; *Mex.* (has vulgar meaning)

mal (mahl) n. evil; adj. bad

malo (MAH-loh) adj. bad; sick

manejar (mah-nay-HAHR) v. manage; drive

mango (MAHN-goh) n. mango

maní (mah-NEE) n. peanuts (except in *Mex.*)

manija (mah-NEE-hah) n. handle

mano (MAH-noh) n. hand

manteca (mahn-TAY-cah) n. lard; *RP* butter

mantecado (mahn-tay-CAH-doh) n. *PR* ice cream

mantener (mahn-tay-NAYR) v. maintain; keep

mantequilla (mahn-tay-KEY-yah) n. butter (except *RP*)

manzana (mahn-SAH-nah) n. apple

mañana (mah-NYAH-nah) n. morning; adv. tomorrow

mapa (MAH-pah) n. map

máquina (MAH-key-nah) n. machine; *Cuba* taxi

máquina de afeitar (MAH-key-nah day ah-fay-TAHR)
    n. razor

mar (mahr) n. sea

marca (MAHR-cah) n. brand

marisco (mah-REES-coh) n. shellfish

martes (MAHR-tays) n. Tuesday

marzo (MAHR-soh) n. March

más (mahs) adv. more; most

matar (mah-TAHR) v. kill

mayo (MAH-yoh) n. May

me (may) pron. me; to me

mecánico (may-CAH-nee-coh) n. mechanic; adj.
    mechanical

medias (MAY-dee-ahs) n. socks

medicina (may-dee-SEE-nah) n. medicine

médico (MAY-dee-coh) n. doctor; adj. medical

medio (MAY-dee-oh) n., adj. half; middle

mediodía (may-dee-oh-DEE-ah) n. noon

medusa (may-DOO-sah) n. *Bol., Uru.* jelly fish

mientras (que) (mee-AYN-trahs kay) conj. while

mejor (may-HOHR) adj. better; best

mejorar (may-hoh-RAHR) v. improve

melocotón (may-loh-coh-TOHN) n. *Carib., Pe.* peach

melón (may-LOHN) n. melon; *Cuba* watermelon

mendigo (mayn-DEE-goh) n. beggar

menor (may-NOHR) adj. less; least; smaller; younger

menos (MAY-nohs) adj., adv. less

mentira (mayn-TEE-rah) n. lie

mercado (mayr-CAH-doh) n. market

merienda (mayr-ree-AYN-dah) n. snack

mercancia (mayr-cahn-SEE-ah) n. merchandise; goods

mermelada (mayr-may-LAH-dah) n. jam

mes (mays) n. month

mesa (MAY-sah) n. table

mesera (may-SAY-rah) n. *Mex.* waitress

mesero (may-SAY-roh) n. *Mex.* waiter

metro (MAY-troh) n. meter (measurement); *Mex.* subway

mi (mee) adj. my

miedo (mee-AY-doh) n. fear

miércoles (mee-AYR-coh-lays) n. Wednesday

mil (meel) n., adj. thousand

milla (MEE-yah) n. mile

millón (mee-YOHN) n. million

minuto (mee-NOO-toh) n. minute

mirar (mee-RAHR) v. look at

mismo (MEES-moh) adj., pron. same

molestar (moh-lays-TAHR) v. bother

momento (moh-MAYN-toh) n. moment

moneda (moh-NAY-dah) n. coin

montaña (mohn-TAH-nyah) n. mountain

morado (moh-RAH-doh) adj. purple

moreno (moh-RAY-noh) adj. dark

morir (moh-REER) v. die

mosca (MOHS-cah) n. fly

mosquito (mohs-KEY-toh) n. mosquito

mostrar (mohs-TRAHR) v. show

motocicleta (moh-toh-see-CLAY-tah) n. motorcycle

motor (moh-TOHR) n. motor; engine

mozo (MOH-soh) n. *Ec., Pe., RP* waiter

muchacha (moo-CHAH-chah) n. girl

muchacho (moo-CHAH-choh) n. boy

mucho (MOO-choh) adj., adv. much

muchos (MOO-chohs) adj., pron. many

muebles (moo-AY-blays) n. furniture

muela (moo-AY-lah) n. molar

muestra (moo-AYS-trah) n. sample

mujer (moo-HAYR) n. woman

mundo (MOON-doh) n. world

museo (moo-SAY-oh) n. museum

música (MOO-see-cah) n. music

muy (MOO-ee) adv. very

¡Muy bien! (MOO-ee bee-AYN) interj. Very well!;
Fine!

N

nacimiento (nah-see-mee-AYN-toh) n. birth

nación (nah-see-OHN) n. nation

nacional (nah-see-oh-NAHL) adj. national

nada (NAH-dah) pron. nothing

nadar (nah-DAHR) v. swim

nadie (NAH-dee-ay) pron. nobody; no one

nafta (NAHF-tah) n. *Arg.* gas

naranja (nah-RAHN-hah) n. orange

nariz (nah-REES) n. nose

Navidad (nah-vee-DAHD) n. Christmas

necesario (nay-say-SAH-ree-oh) adj. necessary

necesitar (nay-say-see-TAHR) v. need

negocio (nay-GOH-see-oh) n. business

negro (NAY-groh) n., adj. black

neumático (nay-oo-MAH-tee-coh) n. *Chi., Uru.* tire

ni (nee) conj. neither

nieto (nee-AY-toh) n. grandson

ninguno (neen-GOO-noh) adj. no; not any; pron. none

niña (NEE-nyah) n. girl

niño (NEE-nyoh) n. boy

no (noh) adv. no; not

noche (NOH-chay) n. night

nombre (NOHM-bray) n. name

norte (NOHR-tay) n. north

nosotros (noh-SOH-trohs) pron. we

nota (NOH-tah) n. note

notar (noh-TAHR) v. note

noticias (noh-TEE-see-ahs) n. news

noventa (noh-VAYN-tah) n., adj. ninety

novia (NOH-vee-ah) n. girlfriend; bride

noviembre (noh-vee-AYM-bray) n. November

novio (NOH-vee-oh) n. boyfriend; groom

nuestro (noo-AYS-troh) adj. our

nueve (noo-AY-vay) n., adj. nine

nuevo (noo-AY-voh) adj. new

número (NOO-may-roh) n. number

nunca (NOON-cah) adv. never

O

o (oh) conj. or; either

objetos de valor (ohb-HAY-tohs day vah-LOHR) n.
    valuables

observar (ohb-sayr-VAHR) v. observe

obtener (ohb-tay-NAYR) v. obtain; get

ochenta (oh-CHAYN-tah) n., adj. eighty

ocho (OH-choh) n., adj. eight

octubre (ok-TOO-bray) n. October

ocupación (oh-coo-pah-see-OHN) n. occupation

ocupar (oh-cooh-PAHR) v. occupy

ocurrir (oh-coo-REER) v. occur; happen

odiar (oh-dee-AHR) v. hate

oeste (oh-AY-stay) n. west

oficial (oh-fee-see-AHL) n. official; officer; adj. official

oficina (oh-fee-SEE-nah) n. office

oficina de correos (oh-fee-SEE-nah day coh-RAY-ohs)
    n. *Mex.* post office

ofrecer (oh-fray-SAYR) v. offer

ofrecimiento (oh-fray-see-mee-AYN-toh) n. offer

oír (oh-EER) v. hear

ojo (OH-hoh) n. eye

olvidar (ohl-vee-DAHR) v. forget

omitir (oh-mee-TEER) v. omit

once (OHN-say) n., adj. eleven

onza (OHN-sah) n. ounce

oportunidad (oh-pohr-too-nee-DAHD) n. opportunity

orden (OHR-dayn) n. order

orden de pago (OHR-dayn day PAH-goh) n. money
    order

organización (ohr-gah-nee-sah-see-OHN) n.
    organization

oro (OH-roh) n. gold

oscuro (ohs-COO-roh) adj. dark

otoño (oh-TOH-nyoh) n. autumn; fall

otra vez (OH-trah vays) adv. again

otro (OH-troh) adj. other; another

P

padre (PAH-dray) n. father; adj. *Mex., Pe.* terrific
    (slang)

padres (PAH-drays) n. parents

pagar (pah-GAHR) v. pay; pay for

página (PAH-hee-nah) n. page

pago (PAH-goh) n. payment

país (pah-EES) n. country; nation

paisaje (pah-ee-SAH-hay) n. landscape

pájaro (PAH-hah-roh) n. bird

pajita (pah-HEE-tah) n. *Chi., Uru.* drinking straw

palabra (pah-LAH-brah) n. word

palomitas (pah-loh-MEE-tahs) n. *Mex.* popcorn

pan (pahn) n. bread

panadería (pah-nah-day-REE-ah) n. bakery

pantalones (pahn-tah-LOHN-nays) n. trousers; pants

papa (PAH-pah) n. potato

papel (pah-PAYL) n. paper

papelería (pah-pay-lay-REE-ah) n. stationery store

paquete (pah-KAY-tay) n. package

para (PAH-rah) prep. to; for

parada (pah-RAH-dah) n. bus stop

paradero (pah-rah-DAY-roh) n. *Chi., Col.* bus stop

paraguas (pah-RAH-gwahs) n. umbrella

pardo (PAHR-doh) adj. brown

parecer (pah-ray-SAYR) v. seem; appear

pared (pah-RAYD) n. wall

pareja (pah-RAY-hah) n. couple

parque (PAHR-kay) n. park

parquear (pahr-kay-AHR) v. *Bol., Cuba* park

parqueo (pahr-KAY-oh) n. *Bol., Cuba* parking lot

parte (PAHR-tay) n. part

participar (pahr-tee-see-PAHR) v. participate

pasado (pah-SAH-doh) n., adj. past

pasador (pah-sah-DOHR) n. *Mex., Uru.* bobby pin

pasajero (pah-sah-HAY-roh) n. passenger

pasamano (pah-sah-MAH-noh) n. handrail

pasaporte (pah-sah-POHR-tay) n. passport

pasar (pah-SAHR) v. pass; *Arg., Ven.* pass (in car)

pasillo (pah-SEE-yoh) n. hall

pastel (pah-STAYL) n. pie; *Mex.* cake

pastelería (pah-stay-lay-REE-ah) n. bakery

patria (PAH-tree-ah) n. homeland

pay (PAH-ee) n. *Mex.* pie

peatón (pay-ah-TOHN) n. pedestrian

pedir (pay-DEER) v. ask for; order

pegamento (pay-gah-MAYN-toh) n. *Mex., Uru.* glue

película (pay-LEE-coo-lah) n. film

peligro (pay-LEE-groh) n. danger

peligroso (pay-lee-GROH-soh) adj. dangerous

pelo (PAY-loh) n. hair

peluquería (pay-loo-kay-REE-ah) n. beauty shop;
    barbershop (except *Cuba*)

peluquero (pay-loo-KAY-roh) n. hairdresser; barber
    (except *Cuba*)

pendientes (payn-dee-AYN-tays) n. *Cuba* dangling
    earrings

pensar (payn-SAHR) n. think

peor (pay-OHR) adj. adv. worse; worst

pepino (pay-PEE-noh) n. cucumber

pequeño (pay-KAY-nyoh) adj. small; *Ven.* short (person)

perchero (payr-CHAY-roh) n. *Cuba* clothes hanger

perder (payr-DAYR) v. lose

perdón (payr-DOHN) n. pardon

perfume (payr-FOO-may) n. perfume

periódico (pay-ree-OH-dee-coh) n. newspaper

perla (PAYR-lah) n. pearl

permiso (payr-MEE-soh) n. permission; permit

permiso de manejo (payr-MEE-soh day mah-NAY-hoh) n. *Arg.* driver's license

permitir (payr-mee-TEER) v. permit

pero (PAY-roh) conj. but

perro (PAY-roh) n. dog

perro caliente (PAY-roh cah-lee-AYN-tay) n. *Cuba, Mex.* hot dog

persona (payr-SOH-nah) n. person

personal (payr-soh-NAHL) n. personnel; adj. personal

pertenecer (payr-tay-nay-SAYR) v. belong

pesca (PAYS-cah) n. fishing

pescado (pays-CAH-doh) n. fish (as food)

pesero (pay-SAY-roh) n. *Mex.* jitney

peso (PAY-soh) n. weight; peso (currency)

petróleo (pay-TROH-lay-oh) n. petroleum; gas

picante (pee-CAHN-tay) adj. hot (spicy)

pico (PEE-coh) n. beak; peak

pie (pee-AY) n. foot

piel (pee-AYL) n. skin

pierna (pee-AYR-nah) n. leg

pieza (pee-AY-sah) n. piece; *Arg.*, *Chi.* room

pijamas (pee-CHAH-mahs) n. pajamas

pila (PEE-lah) n. battery

pimienta (pee-mee-AYN-tah) n. black pepper

pintor (peen-TOHR) n. painter

piña (PEE-nyah) n. pineapple (except *Arg.*)

pipocas (pee-POH-cahs) n. *Bol.* popcorn

pirámide (pee-RAH-mee-day) n. pyramid

piscina (pee-SEE-nah) n. swimming pool (except *Arg.* and *Mex.*)

piso (PEE-soh) n. floor

plancha (PLAHN-chah) n. iron

planta (PLAHN-tah) n. plant

planta baja (PLAHN-tah BAH-hah) n. *Mex.* ground floor

plantar (plahn-TAHR) v. plant

plata (PLAH-tah) n. silver; money (slang)

plátano (PLAH-tah-noh) n. banana

plato (PLAH-toh) n. plate; dish

playa (PLAH-yah) n. beach

plaza mayor (PLAH-sah mah-YOHR) n. main square

pluma (PLOO-mah) n. pen

pobre (POH-bray) adj. poor

poco (POH-coh) adj., pron. little

pocos (POH-cohs) adj., pron. few

poder (poh-DAYR) n. power; v. be able to

policía (poh-lee-SEE-ah) n. police

policía acostado (poh-lee-SEE-ah ah-cohs-TAH-doh) n.
  Ec. speed bumps

política (poh-LEE-tee-cah) n. policy; politics

pollo (POH-yoh) n. chicken

pomelo (poh-MAY-loh) n. *Arg.* grapefruit

poner (poh-NAYR) v. put; place

poner(se) (poh-NAYR-say) v. put on

popotes (poh-POH-tays) n. *Mex.* drinking straws

por (pohr) prep. by; through; by way of

porcentaje (pohr-sayn-TAH-hay) n. percentage

por ciento (pohr see-AYN-toh) adv. percent

porotos (poh-ROH-tohs) n. *Chi.* dry beans

porotos verdes (poh-ROH-tohs VAYR-days) n. *Chi.*
  green beans

porque (POHR-kay) conj. because

¿por qué? (pohr kay) interr. why?

posible (poh-SEE-blay) adj. possible

posición (poh-see-see-OHN) n. position

postre (POH-stray) n. dessert

practicar (prahk-tee-CAHR) v. practice
precio (PRAY-see-oh) n. price
preciso (pray-SEE-soh) adj. necessary
preferir (pray-fay-REER) v. prefer
pregunta (pray-GOON-tah) n. question
preguntar (pray-goon-TAHR) v. ask (question)
preocupar(se) (pray-oh-coo-PAHR-say) v. be worried
preparar (pray-pah-RAHR) v. prepare
presentación (pray-sayn-tah-see-OHN) n. presentation; appearance
presentar (pray-sayn-TAHR) v. present
presidente (pray-see-DAYN-tay) n. president
prestar (pray-STAHR) v. lend
presupuesto (pray-soo-PWAY-stoh) n. budget
primavera (pree-mah-VAY-rah) n. spring
primero (pree-MAY-roh) adj. first
principal (preen-see-PAHL) adj. principal; main
prisión (pree-see-OHN) n. prison
privado (pree-VAH-doh) adj. private
probable (proh-BAH-blay) adj. probable
probar (proh-BAHR) v. prove; try
probar(se) (proh-BAHR-say) v. try on
problema (proh-BLAY-mah) n. problem
producir (proh-doo-SEER) v. produce
producto (proh-DOOK-toh) n. product

profundo (proh-FOON-doh) adj. deep

prohibir (proh-ee-BEER) v. prohibit

promedio (proh-MAY-dee-oh) n. average

prometer (proh-may-TAYR) v. promise

pronto (PROHN-toh) adv. quick; *Uru.* right now

propina (proh-PEE-nah) n. tip

propósito (proh-POH-see-toh) n. purpose

prostituta (proh-stee-TOO-tah) n. prostitute

protección (proh-tayk-see-OHN) n. protection

próximo (PROKH-see-moh) adj. next

público (POO-blee-coh) n. public; audience; adj. public

pueblo (PWAY-bloh) n. people; town

puente (PWAYN-tay) n. bridge

puerta (PWAYR-tah) n. door

puerto (PWAYR-toh) n. port

pulgada (pool-GAH-dah) n. inch

pulsera (pool-SAY-rah) n. bracelet

puntual (poon-too-AHL) adj. punctual

puro (POO-roh) n. *Mex. Pe.* cigar; adj. pure

Q

que (kay) pron. that; which; who; whom

¿qué? (kay) adj., pron. What? Which?

quedar(se) (kay-DAHR-say) v. remain

81

quejar (kay-HAHR) v. complain

quemar (kay-MAHR) v. burn

querer (kay-RAYR) v. wish; want; love

queso (KAY-soh) n. cheese

¿quién? (key-AYN) interr. Who? Whom?

quince (KEYN-say) n., adj. fifteen

quitar (key-TAHR) v. take away

quitar(se) (key-TAHR-say) v. take off

quizás (key-SAHS) adv. perhaps

R

radio (RAH-dee-oh) n. radio

rápido (RAH-pee-doh) adj. fast

rasurar (rah-soo-RAHR) v. *Mex.* shave

rayos X (RAH-yohs AYK-ees) n. X-rays

realmente (ray-ahl-MAYN-tay) adv. really

recado (ray-CAH-doh) n. message

recámara (ray-CAH-mah-rah) n. *Mex.* bedroom

receta (ray-SAY-tah) n. prescription; recipe

recibir (ray-see-VEER) v. receive

recibo (ray-SEE-boh) n. receipt

reciente (ray-see-AYN-tay) adj. recent

reclamar (ray-clah-MAHR) v. claim

recoger (ray-coh-HAYR) v. pick up

recomendar (ray-coh-mayn-DAHR) n. recommend

reconocer (ray-coh-noh-SAYR) v. recognize

reconocimiento (ray-coh-noh-see-mee-AYN-toh) n.
recognition

recordar (ray-cohr-DAHR) v. remember

recuerdo (ray-KWAYR-doh) n. memory; souvenir

referir (ray-fay-REER) v. refer

refresco (ray-FRAYS-coh) n. soft drink

regalo (ray-GAH-loh) n. gift

regatear (ray-gah-tay-AHR) v. bargain

regateo (ray-gah-TAY-oh) n. bargaining

registro (ray-HEE-stroh) n. registration

regresar (ray-gray-SAHR) v. return

rehusar (ray-oo-SAHR) v. refuse

reloj (ray-LOH) n. clock; watch

remitir (ray-mee-TEER) v. forward

remolacha (ray-moh-LAH-chah) n. beet (except *Mex.*)

repetir (ray-pay-TEER) v. repeat

reservación (ray-sayr-vah-see-OHN) n. reservation

reservar (ray-sayr-VAHR) v. reserve

resfriado (rays-free-AH-doh) n. head cold

resolver (ray-sohl-VAYR) v. resolve

responder (rays-pohn-DAYR) v. respond

responsable (rays-pohn-SAH-blay) adj. responsible

respuesta (rays-PWAY-stah) n. reply

restaurante (rays-tah-oo-RAHN-tay) n. restaurant

retraso (ray-TRAH-soh) n. delay

reunión (ray-oo-nee-OHN) n. meeting

revelar (ray-vay-LAHR) v. develop (film)

revista (ray-VEE-stah) n. magazine

rico (REE-coh) adj. rich; delicious

río (REE-oh) n. river

risa (REE-sah) n. laughter

robar (roh-BAHR) v. rob; steal

rodilla (roh-DEE-yah) n. knee

rojo (ROH-hoh) n., adj. red

romper (rohm-PAYR) v. break

ron (rohn) n. rum

ropa (ROH-pah) n. clothes

ropa interior (ROH-pah een-tay-ree-OHR) n. underwear

rosado (roh-SAH-doh) n., adj. pink

rositas de maíz (roh-SAY-tahs day mah-EES) n. *Cuba*
   popcorn

roto (ROH-toh) adj. broken

rubí (roo-BEE) n. ruby

rubio (ROO-bee-oh) n., adj. blond; fair complected
   (person)

rueda (roo-AY-dah) n. wheel

ruido (roo-EE-doh) n. noise
ruta (ROO-tah) n. route

S

sábado (SAH-bah-doh) n. Saturday
sábana (SAH-bah-nah) n. sheet
saber (sah-BAYR) v. know; know how to
sabroso (sah-BROH-soh) adj. delicious
sacar foto (sah-CAHR FOH-toh) v. take a picture
sal (sahl) n. salt
sala (SAH-lah) n. *Cuba, Mex., Uru.* living room
salario (sah-LAH-ree-oh) n. wages
salchicha (sahl-CHEE-chah) n. sausage; *Mex.* frankfurter
salida (sah-LEE-dah) n. exit; departure
salir (sah-LEER) v. come out; leave
salón de belleza (sah-LOHN day bay-YAY-sah) n.
    beauty shop
salsa (SAHL-sah) n. sauce; *Carib.* tropical dance music
salsa picante (SAHL-sah pee-CAHN-tay) n. chilli sauce
saltar (sahl-TAHR) v. jump
salud (sah-LOOD) n. health
saludar (sah-loo-DAHR) v. greet
saludo (sah-LOO-doh) n. greeting
salvar (sahl-VAHR) v. save

sánduche (SAHN-doo-chay) n. *Ec.* sandwich

sandwich (SAHND-oo-eech) n. sandwich

sano (SAH-noh) adj. healthy

satisfactorio (sah-tees-fahk-TOH-ree-oh) adj.
   satisfactory

saya (SAH-yah) n. *Cuba* skirt

seco (SAY-coh) adj. dry

secretario (say-cray-TAH-ree-oh) n. secretary

seda (SAY-dah) n. silk

seguir (say-GHEER) v. follow; continue

según (say-GOON) prep. according to

seguramente (say-goo-ree-MAYN-tay) adv. surely

seguridad (say-goo-ree-DAHD) n. security

seguro (say-GOO-roh) adj. sure; safe

seguro de vida (say-GOO-roh day VEE-dah) n. life
   insurance

seis (says) n., adj. six

selva (SAYL-vah) n. jungle; woods

sello (SAY-yoh) n. stamp; seal

semana (say-MAH-nah) n. week

sencillo (sayn-SEE-yoh) adj. simple; single

sentar (sayn-TAHR) v. seat

sentar(se) (sayn-TAHR-say) v. sit down

sentir(se) (sayn-TEER-say) v. feel; be sorry

señor (say-NYOHR) n. sir; Mr.

señora (say-NYOH-rah) n. Mrs.

señorita (say-nyoh-REE-tah) n. Miss; young lady

separación (say-pah-rah-see-OHN) n. separation

separado (say-pah-RAH-doh) adj. separate

separar (say-pah-RAHR) v. separate

septiembre (sayp-tee-AYM-bray) n. September

ser (sayr) n. being; essence; v. be

servicio (sayr-VEE-see-oh) n. service; restroom

servilleta (sayr-vee-YAY-tah) n. napkin

servir (sayr-VEER) v. serve

sesenta (say-SAYN-tah) n., adj. sixty

setenta (say-TAYN-tah) n., adj. seventy

si (see) conj. if; whether

sí (see) adv. yes; indeed

siempre (see-AYM-pray) adv. always

siesta (see-AY-stah) n. midday rest

siete (see-AY-tay) n., adj. seven

silla (SEE-yah) n. chair

simpático (seem-PAH-tee-coh) adj. nice; charming

sin (seen) prep. without

sindicato (seen-dee-CAH-toh) n. labor union

sin embargo (seen aym-BAHR-goh) adv. nevertheless

sirvienta (seer-vee-AYN-tah) n. maid

sirviente (seer-vee-AYN-tay) n. servant

sistema (sees-TAY-mah) n. system

sobre (SOH-bray) prep. on; upon

sobrepeso (soh-bray-PAY-soh) n. overweight

sociedad (soh-see-ay-DAHD) n. society; company

socio (SOH-see-oh) n. partner; *Cuba* buddy

¡Socorro! (soh-COH-roh) imper. Help!

sol (sohl) n. sun

solamente (soh-lah-MAYN-tay) adv. only

solo (SOH-loh) adj. only; alone

soltero(a) (sohl-TAY-roh/rah) n., adj. single

sombrero (sohm-BRAY-roh) n. hat

sopa (SOH-pah) n. soup

sótano (SOH-tah-noh) n. basement

su (soo) adj. his; her; its; their; your; one's

subir (soo-VEER) v. go up

subterráneo (soob-tay-RAH-nay-oh) n. *Arg., Bol.*
   subway

suciedad (soo-see-ay-DAHD) n. dirt

sucio (SOO-see-oh) adj. dirty

sucursal (soo-coor-SAHL) n. (com.) branch

sudamericano (sood-ah-may-ree-CAH-noh) n., adj.
   South American

suela (SWAY-lah) n. sole of shoe

sueldo (SWAYL-doh) n. salary

sueño (SWAY-nyo) n. dream; sleep

suerte (SWAYR-tay) n. luck

suéter (SWAY-tayr) n. sweater

sumamente (soo-mah-MAYN-tay) adv. extremely

sur (soor) n. south

T

tabaco (tah-BAH-coh) n. tobacco; *CA, Cuba, Ven.* cigar

tacón (tah-COHN) n. heel

tacho (TAH-choh) n. *Arg.* taxi

tal (tahl) adj. such; such a

tal vez (tahl vays) adv. perhaps

tamaño (tah-MAH-nyoh) n. size

también (tahm-bee-AYN) adv. too; also

tan pronto como (tahn-PROHN-toh COH-moh) conj. as soon as

tapa (TAH-pah) n. cover; lid

tapete (tah-PAY-tay) n. *Mex.* throw rug

taquilla (tah-KEY-yah) n. box office; *CR* tavern

tarde (TAHR-day) n. afternoon; adv. late

tarifa (tah-REE-fah) n. tariff; fare

tarjeta (tahr-HAY-tah) n. card

trajeta de presentación (tahr-HAY-tah day pray-sayn-tah-see-OHN) n. business card

tarjeta postal (tahr-HAY-tah pohs-TAHL) n. postcard

taxi (TAHK-see) n. taxi

taza (TAH-sah) n. cup; toilet bowl

tazón (tah-SOHN) n. bowl

té (tay) n. tea

teatro (tay-AH-troh) n. theater

técnico (TAYK-nee-coh) n. technician; adj. technical

tela (TAY-lah) n. cloth

teléfono (tay-LAY-foh-noh) n. telephone

telegrama (tay-lay-GRAH-mah) n. telegram

temblor (taym-BLOHR) n. earthquake

temperatura (taym-pay-rah-too-rah) n. temperature

temprano (taym-PRAH-noh) adj., adv. early

tenedor (tay-nay-DOHR) n. fork

tener (tay-NAYR) v. have; own

tener hambre (tay-NAYR AHM-bray) v. be hungry

tener que (tay-NAYR kay) v. have to; must

tener sed (tay-NAYR sayd) v. be thirsty

tenis (TAY-nees) n. tennis

ternera (tayr-NAY-rah) n. veal

terrible (tay-REE-blay) adj. terrible

tiburón (tee-boo-ROHN) n. shark

tiempo (tee-AYM-poh) n. time; weather

tienda (tee-AYN-dah) n. store; *Pe.* department store

tienda de campaña (tee-AYN-dah day cahm-PAH-nyah) n. tent

tienda de departamentos (tee-AYN-dah day day-pahr-tah-MAYN-tohs) n. department store

tierra (tee-AY-rah) n. land; earth

tijeras (tee-HAY-rahs) n. scissors

timbre (TEEM-bray) n. bell; *Mex.* postage stamp

tina (TEE-nah) n. *Mex.* bathtub

típico (TEE-pee-coh) adj. typical

tipo de cambio (TEE-poh day CAHM-bee-oh) n. rate of exchange

tirar (tee-RAHR) v. pull

toalla (toh-AH-yah) n. towel

tobillo (toh-BEE-yoh) n. ankle

tocar (toh-CAHR) v. touch; knock; play (instrument)

tocino (toh-SEE-noh) n. bacon

todavía (toh-dah-VEE-ah) adv. still; yet

todo (TOH-doh) adj. all; every

todo el mundo (TOH-doh el MOON-doh) pron. everybody

tomate (toh-MAH-tay) n. tomato

tomar (toh-MAHR) v. take; eat; drink

topes (TOH-pays) n. *Mex.* speed bumps

toronja (toh-ROHN-hah) n. grapefruit

torta (TOHR-tah) n. *Arg.* pie; *Ec.* cake; *Mex.* sandwich on roll; *Uru.* pancake

tortilla (tohr-TEE-yah) n. tortilla; *Cuba* omelet

trabajar (trah-bah-HAHR) v. work

trabajo (trah-BAH-hoh) n. work

traducción (trah-dook-see-OHN) n. translation

traducir (trah-doo-SEER) v. translate

traer (trah-AYR) v. bring

tráfico (TRAH-fee-coh) n. traffic

traje (TRAH-hay) n. suit

tranquilo (trahn-KEY-loh) adj. calm; peaceful

trece (TRAY-say) n., adj. thirteen

treinta (TRAYN-tah) n., adj. thirty

tren (trayn) n. train

tres (trays) n., adj. three

trinche (TREEN-chay) n. *Andes, Mex.* fork

triste (TREE-stay) adj. sad

trucha (TROO-chah) n. trout

tu (too) adj. your (familiar)

tú (too) pron. you (familiar)

U

último (OOL-tee-moh) adj. last

un (oon) masc. art. a; an

una (OON-ah) fem. art. a; an

una vez (OON-ah vays) adv. once

universidad (oo-nee-vayr-see-DAHD) n. university

urbano (oor-BAH-noh) adj. urban

urgente (oor-HAYN-tay) adj. urgent

usar (oo-SAHR) v. use

uso (OO-soh) n. use

usted (oo-STAY) pron. sing. you

ustedes (oo-STAY-days) pron. plu. you

usual (oo-soo-AHL) adj. usual

útil (OO-teel) adj. useful

uva (OO-vah) n. grape

V

vacancia (vah-CAHN-see-ah) n. vacancy

vacío (vah-SEE-oh) adj. empty

vago (VAH-goh) adj. *Cuba* lazy

vainilla (vah-ee-NEE-yah) n. vanilla

valer (vah-LAYR) v. be worth

válido (VAH-lee-doh) adj. valid

valioso (vah-lee-OH-soh) adj. valuable

valor (vah-LOHR) n. value; courage

valores (vah-LOH-rays) n. valuables

varios (VAH-ree-ohs) adj. various

vaso (VAH-soh) n. drinking glass

vegetal (vay-hay-TAHL) n., adj. vegetable

veinte (VAYN-tay) n., adj. twenty

vela (VAY-lah) n. candle

velocidad (vay-loh-see-DAHD) n. speed

vencido (vayn-SEE-doh) adj. expired

vendedor (vayn-day-DOHR) n. salesman

vender (vayn-DAYR) v. sell

venir (vay-NEER) v. come

venta (VAYN-tay) n. sale; *SA* grocery store

venta al mayoreo (VAYN-tah ahl mah-yoh-RAY-oh) n.
    wholesale

venta al menudeo (VAYN-tah ahl may-noo-DAY-oh)
    n. retail

ventaja (vayn-TAH-hah) n. advantage

ventana (vay-TAH-nah) n. window

ver (vayr) v. see

verano (vay-RAH-noh) n. summer

verdadero (vayr-dah-DAY-roh) adj. true; real

verde (VAYR-day) n., adj. green

vestido (vay-STEE-doh) n. dress

viajar (vee-ah-HAHR) v. travel

viaje (vee-AH-hay) n. trip

vida (VEE-dah) n. life

viejo (vee-AY-hoh) n. old man; adj. old

viento (vee-AYN-toh) n. wind

viernes (vee-AYR-nays) n. Friday

vino (VEE-noh) n. wine

vino de Jerez (VEE-noh day hay-RAYS) n. sherry

visa (VEE-sah) n. visa

visitante (vee-see-TAHN-tay) n. visitor

visitar (vee-see-TAHR) v. visit

vista (VEE-stah) n. view

víveres (VEE-vay-rays) n. groceries

vivir (vee-VEER) v. live

volar (voh-LAHR) v. fly

volver (vohl-VAYR) v. return

vomitar (voh-mee-TAHR) v. vomit

vos (vohs) pron. *SA*, used instead of fam. *tú* you

vuelo (VWAY-loh) n. flight

W

whisky (same as in English)

X

xilófono (see-LOH-foh-noh) n. xylophone

Y

y (ee) conj. and
ya (yah) adv. already; now
yate (YAH-tay) n. yacht
yo (yoh) pron. I

Z

zapato (sah-PAH-toh) n. shoe
zócalo (SOH-cah-loh) n. *Mex.* main square
zona (SOH-nah) n. zone
zipper (SEE-payr) n. zipper
zoológico (soh-LOH-hee-coh) n. zoo

ENGLISH-SPANISH DICTIONARY

A

a art. un; una (oon; OO-nah)

aboard adv. a bordo (ah BOHR-doh)

abroad adv. en el extranjero (ayn el ex-trahn-HAY-roh)

absolutely adv. absolutamente (ahb-soh-loo-tah-MAYN-tay)

accelerate v. acelerar (ah-say-lay-RAHR)

accent n. acento (ah-SAYN-toh)

accept v. aceptar (ah-sayp-TAHR)

accident n. accidente (ahk-see-DAYN-tay)

according to prep. según (say-GOON)

account n. cuenta (coo-AYN-tah)

accountant n. contador (cohn-tah-DOHR)

acknowledge v. reconocer (ray-coh-noh-SAYR)

acknowledgement n. reconocimiento (ray-coh-noh-see-mee-AYN-toh)

across prep. a través de (ah trah-VAYS day)

act n. acto (AHK-toh)

action n. acción (ahk-see-OHN)

activity n. actividad (ahk-tee-vee-DAHD)

actor n. actor (ahk-TOHR)

actually adv. realmente (ray-ahl-MAYN-tay)

additional adj. adicional (ah-dee-see-oh-NAHL)

address n. dirección (dee-rayk-see-OHN)

admission n. admisión (ahd-mee-see-OHN)

admit v. admitir (ahd-mee-TEEHR)

advance n. avance v. avanzar (ah-vahn-say; ah-vahn-SAHR)

advantage n. ventaja (vayn-TAH-hah)

advertisement n. anuncio comercial (ah-NOON-see-oh coh-mayr-see-AHL)

advice n. consejo (cohn-SAY-hoh)

after adv. después; prep. después de (days-poo-AYS day)

afternoon n. tarde (TAHR-day)

again adv. otra vez (OH-trah vays)

against prep. contra (COHN-trah)

age n. edad (ay-DAHD)

agency n. agencia (ah-HAYN-see-ah)

agent n. agente (ah-HAYN-tay)

ago adv. hace… (time period) (AH-say…)

agreement n. acuerdo (ah-KUAYR-doh)

air n. aire (AH-ee-ray)

air conditioning n. aire acondicionado; *Mex.* clima (AH-ee-ray ah-cohn-dee-see-oh-NAH-doh; CLEE-mah)

airplane n. avión (ah-vee-OHN)

airport n. aeropuerto (ah-ay-roh-PWAYR-toh)

alarm clock n. despertador (days-payr-tah-DOHR)

alcohol n. alcohol (ahl-COHL)

all adj., pron. todo (TOH-doh)

allow v. permitir (payr-mee-TEEHR)

all right adj., adv. está bien (ays-TAH bee-AYN)

almost adv. casi (CAH-see)

alone adj. solo; adv. solamente (SOH-loh; soh-lah-MAYN-tay)

already adv. ya (yah)

also adv. también (tahm-bee-AYN)

although conj. aunque; sin embargo (ah-OON-kay; seen aym-BAHR-goh)

altitude n. altura (ahl-TOO-rah)

always adv. siempre (see-AYM-pray)

ambassador n. embajador (aym-bah-hah-DOHR)

amber n. ámbar (AHM-bahr)

ambulance n. ambulancia (ahm-boo-LAHN-see-ah)

among prep. entre (AYN-tray)

amount n. cantidad (cahn-tee-DAHD)

amuse v. divertir (dee-vayr-TEER)

an art. un; una (oon; OO-nah)

ancient adj. antiguo (ahn-TEE-gwoh)

and conj. y (ee)

angry adj. enojado (ayn-oh-HAH-doh)

ankle n. tobillo (toh-BEE-yoh)

announce v. anunciar (ah-noon-see-AHR)

annoy v. molestar (moh-lays-TAHR)

annual adj. anual (ah-noo-AHL)

another adj. otro (OH-troh)

answer n. respuesta; v. contestar (rays-PWAY-stah; cohn-tays-TAHR)

antique n. antigüedad (ahn-tee-gway-DAHD)

any pron., adj. alguno (ahl-GOO-noh)

anybody pron. alguien (AHL-ghee-ayn)

anything pron. cualquier cosa (kwal-key-AHR COH-sah)

apart adv. aparte (ah-PAHR-tay)

apartment n. apartamento; *Mex.* departamento (ah-pahr-tah-MAYN-toh; day-pahr-tah-MAYN-toh)

appearance n. presentación (pray-sayn-tah-see-OHN)

apple n. manzana (mahn-SAHN-ah)

appointment n. cita (SEE-tah)

area n. área (AH-ree-ah)

argue v. discutir (dees-coo-TEER)

arm n. brazo (BRAH-soh); (mil.) arma (AHR-mah)

around adv. alrededor (ahl-ray-day-DOHR)

arrange v. arreglar (ah-ray-GLAHR)

arrival n. llegada (yay-GAH-dah)

arrive v. llegar (yay-GAHR)

art n. arte (AHR-tay)

artist n. artista (ahr-TEES-tah)

as conj. como (COH-moh)

ashtray n. cenicero (say-nee-SAY-roh)

ask v. preguntar (pray-goon-TAHR)

ask for v. pedir (pay-DEER)

assets n. capital; (pl.) valores (cah-pee-TAHL; vah-LOH-rays)

assist v. ayudar (ah-yoo-DAHR)

assistant n. asistente (ah-sees-TAYN-tay)

associate n. socio (SOH-see-oh)

as soon as conj. tan pronto como (tahn PROHN-toh COH-moh)

as well as conj. así como (ah-SEE COH-moh)

at prep. a; en (ah;ayn)

at home adv. en casa (ayn CAH-sah)

at least adv. al menos (ahl MAY-nohs)

at once adv. en seguida (ayn say-GHEE-dah)

attempt v. intentar (een-tayn-TAHR)

attend v. asistir (ah-sees-TEER)

at times adv. a veces (ah VAY-says)

attorney n. abogado; *Arg.* boga; *Mex.* licenciado (ah-boh-GAH-doh; BOH-gah; lee-sayn-see-AH-doh)

aunt n. tía (TEE-ah)

automatic adj. automático (ah-oo-toh-MAH-tee-coh)

autumn n. otoño (oh-TOH-nyoh)

available adj. disponible (dees-pohn-EE-blay)

avenue n. avenida (ah-vay-NEE-dah)

average n. promedio (proh-MAY-dee-oh)

avoid v. evitar (ay-vee-TAHR)

awful adj. terrible; horrible (tay-REE-blay; oh-REE-blay)

B

baby n. bebé; *Chi., Ec.* guagua (bay-BAY; GWAH-gwah)

bacon n. tocino (toh-SEE-noh)

bad adj. mal; malo (mahl; MAH-loh)

bag n. bolsa (BOHL-sah)

baggage n. equipaje (ay-key-PAH-hay)

bakery n. panadería (pah-nah-day-REE-ah)

banana n. plátano; *PR* guineo; *Ven.* cambur (PLAH-tah-noh; ghee-NAY-oh; cahm-BOOR)

bank n. banco (BAHN-coh)

bar n. bar (bahr)

barber n. barbero; *Arg., Mex., Uru.* peluquero (bahr-BAY-roh; pay-loo-KAY-roh)

bargain n. ganga v. regatear; *Chi.* pelear el precio (GAHN-gah; ray-gah-tay-AHR)

bargaining n. regateo (ray-gah-TAY-oh)

basis n. base (BAH-say)

basket n. canasta (cah-NAHS-tah)

bath n. baño (BAH-nyoh)

bathe v. bañar; bañar(se) (bah-NYARH; bah-NYAHR-say)

bathroom n. sala de baño; baño (SAH-lah day BAH-nyoh)

bathtub n. bañera; *Arg., Cuba* bañadera; *Mex.* tina (bah-NYAY-rah; bah-nyah-DAY-rah; TEE-nah)

battery n. batería; pila (bah-tay-REE-ah; PEE-lah)

be v. ser; estar (sayr; ays-TAHR)

be able v. poder (poh-DAYR)

beach n. playa (PLAH-yah)

be afraid v. tener miedo (tay-NAYR mee-AY-doh)

beak n. pico (PEE-coh)

beans (dry) n. *Arg., Bol., Chi., Ec., Uru.* porotos; *Cuba, Mex.* frijoles (poh-ROH-tohs; free-HOH-lays)

beautiful adj. hermoso; bello (ayr-MOH-soh; BAY-yoh)

beauty shop n. salón de belleza; peluquería (sah-LOHN day bay-YAY-sah; pay-loo-kay-REE-ah)

because conj. porque (POHR-kay)

bed n. cama (CAH-mah)

bedroom n. cuarto de dormir; *Arg., Chi.* pieza; *Cuba, Uru., Ven.* habitación; *Mex.* recámara; *Uru.* cuarto (KWAHR-toh de dohr-MEER; pee-AY-sah; ah-bee-tah-see-OHN; ray-CAH-mah-rah; KWAHR-toh)

beef n. carne de res (CAHR-nay day rays)

beefsteak n. bistec; *RP* bife (bees-TAYK; BEE-fay)

beer n. cerveza (sayr-VAY-sah)

beet n. remolacha; *Mex.* betabel (ray-moh-LAH-chah; bay-tah-BAYL)

before prep., adv. ante; conj. antes de que (AHN-tay; AHN-tays day kay)

beggar n. mendigo (mayn-DEE-goh)

begin v. empezar; comenzar (aym-pay-SAHR; coh-mayn-SAHR)

behind prep. adv. detrás (day-TRAHS)

be hungry v. tener hambre (tay-NAYR AHM-bray)

believe v. creer (cray-AYR)

bell n. timbre (TEEM-bray)

bellhop n. botones (boh-TOH-nays)

belong v. pertenecer (payr-tay-nay-SAYR)

below adv. debajo; prep. debajo de (day-BAH-hoh day)

belt n. cinturón (seen-too-ROHN)

be right v. tener razón (tay-NAYR rah-SOHN)

beside prep. al lado de (ahl LAH-doh day)

be sorry v. sentir(se) (sayn-TEER-say)

best adj. mejor (may-HOHR)

be thirsty v. tener sed (tay-NAYR sayd)

better adv. mejor (may-HOHR)

between prep. entre (AYN-tray)

beverage n. bebida (bay-BEE-dah)

be worth v. valer (vah-LAYR)

be wrong v. equivocar(se) (ah-kee-voh-CAHR-say)

bicycle n. bicicleta (bee-see-CLAY-tah)

big adj. grande (GRAHN-day)

bill n. cuenta; (money) billete (coo-AYN-tah; bee-YAY-tay)

bird n. pájaro (PAH-hah-roh)

birth n. nacimiento (nah-see-mee-AYN-toh)

birthday n. cumpleaños (coom-play-AHN-yohs)

black adj. negro (NAY-groh)

block n. cuadra (KWAH-drah)

blond n., adj. rubio; *Mex.* güero (ROO-bee-oh; GWAY-roh)

blouse n. blusa (BLOO-sah)

blue n., adj. azul (ah-SOOL)

boat n. barco (BAHR-coh)

bobby pin n. *Ec.* imperdible; *Mex., Uru.* pasador; *Pan.*
    gancho (eem-payr-DEE-blay; pah-sah-DOHR;
    GHAN-choh)

body n. cuerpo (coo-AYR-poh)

book n. libro (LEE-broh)

bookstore n. librería (lee-bray-REE-ah)

border n. frontera (frohn-TAY-rah)

bottle n. botella (boh-TAY-yah)

bowl n. *Arg., Bol., Mex.* tazón; *Ven.* taza (tah-SOHN;
    TAH-sah)

box n. caja (CAH-hah)

box office n. taquilla (tah-KEY-yah)

boy n. niño; muchacho (NEE-nyoh; moo-CHAH-choh)

boyfriend n. novio; *Ven.* empate (NOH-vee-oh; aym-
    PAH-tay)

bracelet n. pulsera; *Ven.* brazalete (pool-SAY-rah;
    brah-sah-LAY-tay)

branch n. sucursal (soo-coor-SAHL)

brand n. marca (MAHR-cah)

bread n. pan (pahn)

break v. romper (rohm-PAYR)

breakfast n. desayuno (day-sah-YOO-noh)

bridge n. puente (PWAYN-tay)

brief adj. breve (BRAY-vay)

bring v. traer (trah-AYR)

broad adj. ancho (AHN-choh)

broken adj. roto (ROH-toh)

brother n. hermano (ayr-MAH-noh)

brown adj. pardo; *Mex.* café (PAHR-doh; cah-FAY)

buddy n. *Arg., Bol., Uru.* compinche; *Cuba* socio; *Mex.* cuate (cohm-PEEN-chay; SOH-see-oh; KWAH-tay)

budget n. presupuesto (pray-soo-PWAYS-toh)

bug n. insecto; bicho (vulgar in *PR*) (een-SAYK-toh; BEE-choh)

bulb n. bombilla; *Mex.* foco (bohm-BEE-yah; FOH-coh)

burn v. quemar (kay-MAHR)

bus (city) n. *Arg., Bol.* colectivo; *Carib.* guagua; *Mex.* camión (coh-layk-TEE-voh; GWAH-gwah; cah-mee-OHN)

bus (intercity) n. *Caribe, Mex.* autobús (ah-oo-toh-BOOS)

business n. negocio (nay-GOH-see-oh)

business card n. tarjeta de presentación (tahr-HAY-tah day pray-sayn-tah-see-OHN)

businessman n. hombre de negocios (OHM-bray de nay-GOH-see-ohs)

bus stop n. parada; *Chi., Col.* paradero (pah-RAH-dah; par-rah-DAY-roh)

but conj. pero (PAY-roh)

butter n. mantequilla; *Arg.* manteca (mahn-tay-KEY-yah; mahn-TAY-cah)

button n. botón (boh-TOHN)

buy v. comprar (cohm-PRAHR)

buyer n. comprador (cohm-prah-DOHR)

by prep. por (pohr)

C

cab n. taxi; *Arg.* tacho; *Cuba* máquina (TAHK-see; TAH-choh)

cake n. *Chi., Ec., Uru.* torta; *Mex.* pastel; *PR* bizcocho (tohr-tah; pah-STAYL; bees-COH-choh)

calendar n. calendario (cah-layn-DAH-ree-oh)

call n. llamada; v. llamar (yah-MAH-dah; yah-MAHR)

camera n. cámara (CAH-mah-rah)

camp n. campamento (cahm-pah-MAYN-toh)

can n. lata; v. poder (LAH-tah; poh-DAYR)

candle n. vela (VAY-lah)

candy n. dulces (DOOL-says)

canyon n. cañón (cah-NYOHN)

capital n. capital (cah-pee-TAHL)

car n. auto; carro; coche (AH-oo-toh; CAH-roh; COH-chay)

carburetor n. carburador (cahr-boo-rah-DOHR)

card n. tarjeta (tahr-HAY-tah)

care for v. cuidar (coo-ee-DAHR)

careful adj. cuidadoso (coo-ee-dah-DOH-soh)

cargo n. carga; cargamento (CAHR-gah; cahr-gah-MAYN-toh)

carry v. llevar (yay-VAHR)

cart n. carreta (cah-RAY-tah)

case n. caso (KAH-soh)

cash n. efectivo (ay-FAYKT-tee-voh)

cashier n. cajero (cah-HAYR-roh)

cat n. gato (GAH-toh)

catch up v. alcanzar (ahl-cahn-SAHR)

cathedral n. catedral (cah-tay-DRAHL)

cause n. causa; v. causar (CAH-oo-sah; cah-oo-SAHR)

cave n. cueva (coo-AY-vah)

cellar n. sótano (SOH-tah-noh)

cent n. centavo (sayn-TAH-voh)

central adj. central (sayn-TRAHL)

central heating n. calefacción (cah-lay-fahk-see-OHN)

ceramics n. cerámica (say-RAH-mee-cah)

certainly adv. seguramente (say-goo-rah-MAYN-tay)

certificate n. certificado (sayr-tee-fee-CAH-doh)

chair n. silla (SEE-yah)

champagne n. champaña (chahm-APH-nyah)

change n. cambio; v. cambiar (CAHM-bee-oh; cahm-bee-AHR)

charge v. cobrar (coh-BRAHR)

cheap adj. barato (bah-RAH-toh)

check n. cheque (bank); cuenta (restaurant) (CHAY-kay; coo-AYN-tah)

cheese n. queso (KAY-soh)

chewing gum n. chicle (CHEE-clay)

chicken n. pollo (POH-yoh)

child n. niño; niña (fem.) (NEE-nyoh; NEE-nyah)

chilli n. chile; *SA* aji (CHEE-lay; ah-HEE)

chilli sauce n. salsa picante (SAHL-sah pee-CAHN-tay)

chocolate n. chocolate (choh-coh-LAH-tay)

choose v. escoger (ays-coh-HAYR)

chop n. chuleta (choo-LAY-tah)

Christmas n. Navidad (nah-vee-DAHD)

church n. iglesia (ee-GLAY-see-ah)

cigar n. *Cuba, Ven.* tabaco; *Ec., PR* cigarro; *Mex., Pe.* puro (tah-BAH-coh; see-GAH-roh; POO-roh)

cigarette n. cigarrillo; *Cuba, Mex.* cigarro (see-gah-REE-yoh; see-GAH-roh)

cinnamon n. canela (cah-NAY-lah)

circle n. círculo (SEER-coo-loh)

citizen n. ciudadano (see-oo-da-DAH-noh)

city n. ciudad (see-oo-DAHD)

city bus n. *Arg., Bol.* colectivo; *Carib.* guagua; *Mex.* camión (coh-layk-TEE-voh; GWAH-gwah; cah-mee-OHN)

claim n. reclamación; v. reclamar (ray-clah-mah-see-OHN; ray-clah-MAHR)

class n. clase (CLAH-say)

clean adj. limpio; v. limpiar (LEEM-pee-oh; leem-pee-AHR)

clerk n. dependiente; *Arg.* vendedor (day-payn-dee-AYN-tay; vayn-day-DOHR)

climate n. clima (CLEE-mah)

climb v. subir (soo-BEER)

clock n. reloj (ray-LOH)

close v. cerrar, (say-RAHR); adv. cerca (SAYR-cah)

cloth n. tela (TAY-lah)

clothes n. ropa (ROH-pah)

club n. club (cloob)

coffee n. café (cah-FAY)

cognac n. coñac (coh-NYAK)

coin n. moneda (moh-NAY-dah)

cold n., adj. frío (temperature); resfriado (FREE-oh; rays-free-AH-doh)

color n. color (coh-LOHR)

comb n. peine (PAY-nay)

come v. venir (vay-NEER)

come down v. bajar (bah-HAR)

Come in! imper. ¡Pase! (PAH-say)

come in v. entrar; pasar (ayn-TRAHR; pah-SAHR)

come out v. salir (sah-LEER)

comfortable adj. cómodo (COH-moh-doh)

commerce n. comercio (coh-MAYR-see-oh)

commercial adj. comercial (coh-mayr-see-AHL)

commission n. comisión (coh-mee-see-OHN)

companion n. compañero (cohm-pah-NYAY-roh)

company n. compañía (cohm-pah-NYEE-ah)

complain v. quejar(se) (kay-HAR-say)

complete adj. completo (cohm-PLAY-toh)

computer n. computadora (cohm-poo-tah-DOHR-ah)

concert n. concierto (cohn-see-AYR-toh)

conclusion n. conclusión (cohn-cloo-see-OHN)

condition n. condición (cohn-dee-see-OHN)

conference n. congreso (cohn-GRAY-soh)

congratulations n. felicitaciones (fay-lee-see-tah-see-OHN-ays)

congress n. congreso (legis.) (cohn-GRAY-soh)

consider v. considerar (cohn-see-day-RAHR)

consign v. consignar; entregar (cohn-seeg-NAHR; ayn-tray-GAHR)

consignment n. consignación (cohn-seeg-nah-see-OHN)

constant adj. constante (cohn-STAHN-tay)

constitute v. constituir (cohns-stee-too-EER)

consulate n. consulado (cohn-soo-LAH-doh)

consult v. consultar (cohn-sool-TAHR)

contact n. contacto (cohn-TAHK-toh)

contain v. contener (cohn-tay-NAYR)

container n. envase (ayn-VAH-say)

content adj. contento (cohn-TAYN-toh)

contents n. contenido (cohn-tay-NEE-doh)

continue v. continuar (cohn-tee-noo-AHR)

contract n. contrato (cohn-TRAH-toh)

control n. control; v. controlar (cohn-TROHL; cohn-troh-LAHR)

convenient adj. conveniente (cohn-vay-nee-AYN-tay)

converse v. conversar (cohn-vayr-SAHR)

cook n. cocinero; v. cocinar; guisar (coh-see-NAY-roh; coh-see-NAHR; ghee-SAHR)

cool adj. fresco (FRAYS-coh)

copy n. copia; v. copiar (COH-pee-ah; coh-pee-AHR)

corner n. esquina; rincón (ess-KEY-nah; reen-COHN)

corporation n. corporación (cohr-por-rah-see-OHN)

cost n. costo; precio; v. costar (COH-stoh; PRAY-see-oh; coh-STAHR)

cotton n. algodón (ahl-goh-DOHN)

count v. contar (cohn-TAHR)

country n. país (nation); campo (rural area) (pah-EES; CAHM-poh)

cover n. tapa; v. cubrir (TAH-pah; coo-BREER)

cracker n. galleta (gah-YAY-tah)

crash v. chocar (choh-CAHR)

crazy adj. loco (LOH-coh)

credit n. crédito (CRAY-dee-toh)

crime n. crimen (CREE-mayn)

cucumber n. pepino (pay-PEE-noh)

culture n. cultura (cool-TOO-rah)

cup n. taza (TAH-sah)

cure n. cura; v. curar (KOO-rah; koo-RAHR)

current adj. actual (ahk-too-AHL)

curtain n. cortina (cohr-TEE-nah)

curve n. curva (KOOR-vah)

custom duty n. derecho de aduana (day-RAY-choh de ah-DWAH-nah)

customer n. cliente (klee-AYN-tay)

customs n. aduana (ah-DWAH-nah)

cut v. cortar (cohr-TAHR)

D

daily adj. diario (dee-AH-ree-oh)

damage n. daño; v. dañar (DAH-nyoh; dah-NYAHR)

dance n. baile; v. bailar (BAH-ee-lay; bah-ee-LAHR)

danger n. peligro (pay-LEE-groh)

dangerous adj. peligroso (pay-lee-GROH-soh)

dark adj. oscuro (ohs-COO-roh)

date n. fecha; cita (FAY-chah; SEE-tah)

daughter n. hija (EE-hah)

day n. día (DEE-ah)

debt n. deuda (DAY-oo-dah)

December n. diciembre (dee-see-AYM-bray)

decision n. decisión (day-see-dee-OHN)

declare v. declarar (day-clah-RAHR)

deep adj. profundo (proh-FOON-doh)

delay n. retraso (ray-TRAH-soh)

delicious adj. delicioso; sabroso; rico (day-lee-see-OH-soh; sah-BROH-soh; REE-coh)

deliver v. entregar (ayn-tray-GAHR)

demand n. demanda; v. demandar (de-MAHN-dah; de-mahn-DAHR)

demonstrate v. demostrar (day-mohs-TRAHR)

dentist n. dentista (dayn-TEES-tah)

department n. departamento (day-pahr-tah-MAYN-toh)

department store n. almacén; tienda de departamentos (ahl-mah-SAYN; tee-AYN-day day day-pahr-tah-MAYN-tohs)

deposit n. depósito; v. depositar (day-POH-see-toh; day-poh-see-TAHR)

describe v. describir (days-cree-VEER)

description n. descripción (days-creep-see-OHN)

dessert n. postre (POHS-tray)

detail n. detalle (day-TAH-yay)

determine v. determinar (day-tayr-mee-NAHR)

develop v. desarrollar; revelar (photo) (days-ah-roh-YAHR; ray-vay-LAHR)

diamond n. diamante (dee-ah-MAHN-tay)

die v. morir (moh-REER)

difference n. diferencia (dee-fay-RAYN-see-ah)

different adj. diferente (dee-fay-RAYN-tay)

dining room n. comedor (coh-may-DOHR)

dinner n. cena; comida (SAY-nah; coh-MEE-dah)

direct adj. directo; v. dirigir (dee-RAYK-toh; dee-ree-HEER)

direction n. dirección (dee-rayk-see-OHN)

director n. director (dee-rayk-TOHR)

dirt n. suciedad; *Arg.* roña (soo-see-ay-DAHD; ROH-nyah)

dirty adj. sucio (SOO-see-oh)

discount n. descuento (days-coo-AYN-toh)

discover v. descubrir (days-coo-BREER)

dish n. plato (PLAH-toh)

distance n. distancia (dees-TAHN-see-ah)

distant adj. distante (dees-TAHN-tay)

distribute v. distribuir (dees-tree-boo-EER)

disturb v. molestar (moh-lays-TAHR)

division n. división (dee-vee-see-OHN)

do v. hacer (ah-SAYR)

doctor n. médico; doctor (MAY-dee-coh; dohk-TOHR)

document n. documento (doh-coo-MAYN-toh)

dog n. perro (PAY-roh)

dollar n. dólar (DOH-lahr)

door n. puerta (PWAYR-tah)

double adj. doble (DOH-blay)

doubt n. duda; v. dudar (DOO-dah; doo-DAHR)

dozen n. docena (doh-SAY-nah)

drawer n. cajón (cah-HOHN)

dress n. vestido; v. vestir (vays-TEE-doh; vays-TEER)

drink n. bebida; *Mex.* copa; v. beber; tomar (bay-BEE-dah; COH-pah; bay-BAYR; toh-MAHR)

drive v. manejar; conducir (mah-nay-HAHR; cohn-doo-SEER)

driver n. chofer (choh-FAYR)

drug n. medicamento (may-dee-cah-MAYN-toh)

drugstore n. farmacia; *Cuba* botica (fahr-MAH-see-ah; boh-TEE-cah)

drunk n., adj. borracho (boh-RAH-choh)

dry adj. seco; v. secar (SAY-coh; say-CAHR)

due adj. debido; vencido (day-BEE-doh; vayn-SEE-doh)

during prep. durante (doo-RAHN-tay)

E

each pron., adj. cada (CAH-dah)

early adv. temprano (taym-PRAH-noh)

earn v. ganar (gah-NAHR)

earnings n. ganancias (gah-NAHN-see-ahs)

earrings n. aretes; pendientes; *Arg., Chi.*, aros (ah-RAY-tays; payn-dee-AYN-tays; AH-rohs)

earthquake n. temblor (taym-BLOHR)

easily adv. fácilmente (FAH-seel-mayn-tay)

east n. este (ESS-tay)

easy adj. fácil (FAH-seel)

eat v. comer (coh-MAYR)

economy n. economía (ay-coh-noh-MEE-ah)

efficient adj. eficiente (ay-fee-see-AYN-tay)

egg n. huevo; *Mex.* blanquillo (WAY-voh; blahn-KEY-yoh)

eight n., adj. ocho (OH-choh)

eighteen n., adj. diez y ocho (dee-AYS ee OH-choh)

eighty n., adj. ochenta (oh-CHAYN-tah)

element n. elemento (ay-lay-MAYN-toh)

elevator n. elevador; *SA* ascensor (ay-lay-vah-DOHR; ah-sayn-SOHR)

eleven n., adj. once (OHN-say)

embassy n. embajada (aym-bah-HAH-dah)

embrace n. abrazo; v. abrazar(se) (ah-BRAH-soh; ah-brah-SAHR-say)

emerald n. esmeralda (ess-may-RAHL-dah)

employ v. emplear (aym-play-AHR)

employment n. empleo (aym-PLAY-oh)

empty adj. vacío (vah-SEE-oh)

encounter n. encuentro; v. encontrar (ayn-coo-AYN-troh; ayn-cohn-TRAHR)

end n. fin; v. terminar (feen; tayr-mee-NAHR)

engine n. motor (moh-TOHR)

enough adj., adv. bastante (bah-STAHN-tay)

enter v. entrar (ayn-TRAHR)

enterprise n. empresa (aym-PRAY-sah)

entertainment n. diversión (dee-vayr-see-OHN)

entire adj. entero (ayn-TAY-roh)

entrance n. entrada (ayn-TRAH-dah)

envelope n. sobre (SOH-bray)

equal adj. igual (ee-GWAL)

erase v. borrar (boh-RAHR)

especially adv. especialmente (ays-pay-see-ahl-MAYN-tay)

establish v. establecer (ays-tah-blay-SAYR)

estimate n. presupuesto (pray-soo-PWAY-stoh)

even adv. aún (ah-OON)

evening n. tarde; noche (TAHR-day; NOH-chay)

every adj. todo; cada uno (TOH-doh; CAH-dah OO-noh)

everybody pron. todo el mundo (TOH-doh el MOON-doh)

everything pron. todo (TOH-doh)

everywhere adv. en todas partes (ayn TOH-dahs PAHR-tays)

examination n. examen (ex-AH-mayn)

examine v. examinar (ex-ah-mee-NAHR)

example n. ejemplo (ay-HAYM-ploh)

excellent adj. excelente (ex-say-LAYN-tay)

excess n., adj. exceso (ex-SAY-soh)

exchange n. cambio; v. cambiar (CAHM-bee-oh; cahm-bee-AHR)

excursion n. excursión (ex-coor-see-OHN)

excuse v. perdonar (payr-doh-NAHR)

exhibition n. exhibición (ex-ee-bee-see-OHN)

exit n. salida (sah-LEE-dah)

expect v. esperar (ess-pay-RAHR)

expense n. gasto (GAHS-toh)

expensive adj. caro (CAH-roh)

explain v. explicar (ex-plee-CAHR)

explanation n. explicación (ex-plee-cah-see-OHN)

export v. exportar (ex-pohr-TAHR)

exports n. exportaciones (ex-pohr-tah-see-OHN-ays)

exterior n. exterior; adj. exterior (ex-tay-ree-OHR)

extremely adv. sumamente (soo-mah-MAYN-tay)

eye n. ojo (OH-hoh)

eyeglasses n. anteojos; *Mex.* lentes; *Cuba* espejuelos (ahn-tay-OH-hohs; LAYN-tays; ess-pay-hoo-AY-lohs)

F

fabric n. tela (TAY-lah)

face n. cara (CAH-rah)

fact n. hecho (AY-choh)

factory n. fábrica (FAH-bree-cah)

fail v. fracasar (frah-cah-SAHR)

failure n. fracaso (frah-CAH-soh)

fall n. otoño; v. caer(se) (oh-TOH-nyoh; cah-AYR-say)

family n. familia (fah-MEE-lee-ah)

famous adj. famoso (fah-MOH-soh)

fantastic adj. fantástico (fahn-TAHS-tee-coh)

far adv. lejos (LAY-hohs)

fare n. tarifa (tah-REE-fah)

farm n. granja; *Cuba* finca; *RP* estancia (GRAHN-hah; FEEN-cah; ess-TAHN-see-ah)

fast adj. rápido (RAH-pee-doh)

fat adj. gordo (GOHR-doh)

father n. padre (PAH-dray)

fear n. miedo; v. tener miedo (mee-AY-doh; tay-NAYR mee-AY-doh)

February n. febrero (fay-BRAY-roh)

fee n. honorario (oh-noh-RAH-ree-oh)

feel v. sentir(se) (sayn-TEER-say)

fever n. fiebre; *Mex.* calentura (fee-AY-bray; cah-LAYN-too-rah)

few adj. pocos; algunos (POH-cohs; ahl-GOO-nohs)

fifteen n., adj. quince (KEYN-say)

fifty n., adj. cincuenta (seen-KWAYN-tah)

fight n. lucha; v. luchar (LOO-chah; loo-CHAHR)

file n. archivo (for papers); v. archivar (papers) (ahr-CHEE-voh; ahr-chee-VAHR)

film n. película (pay-LEE-coo-lah)

finance n. finanza; v. financiar (fee-NAHN-sah; fee-nahn-see-AHR)

find v. encontrar (ayn-cohn-TRAHR)

fine! interj. ¡Muy bien! (MOO-ee bee-AYN)

finger n. dedo (DAY-doh)

finish v. terminar (tayr-mee-NAHR)

fire n. fuego; *Cuba*, *Ven.* candela (FWAY-goh; cahn-DAY-lah)

first n., adj., adv. primero (pree-MAY-roh)

fish n. pescado (pays-CAH-doh)

fishing n. pesca (PAYS-cah)

five n., adj. cinco (SEE-coh)

fix v. arreglar (ahr-ray-GLAHR)

flag n. bandera (bahn-DAY-rah)

flight n. vuelo (VWAY-loh)

floor n. piso (PEE-soh)

flower n. flor (flohr)

flu n. gripe; *Mex.* gripa (GREE-pay; GREE-pah)

fly v. volar (voh-LAHR)

follow v. seguir (say-GHEER)

food n. comida (coh-MEE-dah)

foot n. pie (pee-AY)

football (Amer.) n. fútbol americano (FOOT-bohl
  ah-mehr-ee-KHAN-oh)

for prep. por; para (pohr; PAH-rah)

foreign adj. extranjero (ex-trahn-HAY-roh)

forget v. olvidar(se) (ohl-vee-DAHR-say)

fork n. tenedor; *Andes, Mex.* trinche (tay-nay-DOHR;
  TREEN-chay)

form n. forma; v. formar (FOHR-mah; fohr-MAHR)

forty n., adj. cuarenta (kwah-RAYN-tah)

four n., adj. cuatro (KWAH-troh)

fourteen n., adj. catorce (cah-TOHR-say)

free adj. libre; adv. gratis (free of charge) (LEE-bray;
  GRAH-tees)

freedom n. libertad (lee-bayr-TAHD)

freight n. carga; flete (CAHR-gah; FLAY-tay)

frequently adv. frecuentemente (fray-kwayn-tay-
  MAYN-tay)

fresh adj. fresco (FRAYS-coh)

Friday n. viernes (vee-AYR-nays)

friend n. amigo (ah-MEE-goh)

from prep. de; desde (day; DAYS-day)

fruit n. fruta (FROO-tah)

full adj. lleno (YAY-noh)

fund n. fondo (FOHN-doh)
funny adj. cómico (COH-mee-coh)
furniture n. muebles (moo-AY-blays)
future n. futuro (foo-TOO-roh)

G

gallon n. galón (gah-LOHN)
gamble v. apostar (ah-pos-HAR)
gambling n. juegos; apuestos (HWAY-gohs;
    ah-PWAY-stohs)
game n. juego (HWAY-goh)
garage n. garaje; *Mex.* cochera (gah-RAH-hay;
    coh-CHAY-rah)
garbage n. basura (bah-SOO-rah)
garden n. jardín (hahr-DEEN)
garlic n. ajo (AH-hoh)
gas n. gasolina; *Arg.* nafta (gah-soh-LEE-nah; NAHF-tah)
gem n. joya (HOH-yah)
general n. (mil.) general; adj. general (hay-nay-RAHL)
gentleman n. caballero; señor (cah-bah-YAY-roh; say-
    NYOHR)
genuine adj. genuino (hay-noo-EE-noh)
get v. obtener (ohb-tay-NAYR)
gift n. regalo (ray-GAH-loh)
gin n. ginebra (hee-NAY-brah)

girl n. muchacha; niña (moo-CHAH-chah; NEE-nyah)

girlfriend n. novia; *Ven.* empate (NOH-vee-ah; aym-PAH-tay)

give v. dar (dahr)

glass n. vaso (tumbler) (VAH-soh)

glasses n. anteojos; lentes; *Cuba* espejuelos (ahn-tay-OH-hohs; LAYN-tays; ess-pay-hoo-AY-lohs)

glove n. guante (GWAN-tay)

glue n. pegamento; *Cuba, Uru.* goma (pay-gah-MAYN-toh; GOH-mah)

go v. ir (eer)

go away v. ir(se) (EER-say)

go back v. regresar (ray-gray-SAHR)

god n. dios (dee-OHS)

gold n. oro (OH-roh)

golf n. golf (golf)

good adj. bueno (BWAY-noh)

good-bye n. adiós (ah-dee-OHS)

goods n. mercancías (mayr-cahn-SEE-ahs)

go out v. salir (sah-LEER)

go shopping v. ir de compras (eer day COHM-prahs)

government n. gobierno (goh-bee-AYR-noh)

governor n. gobernador (goh-bayr-nah-DOHR)

grandfather n. abuelo (ah-BWAY-loh)

grandmother n. abuela (ah-BWAY-lah)

grandson n. nieto (nee-AY-toh)

grape n. uva (OO-vah)

grapefruit n. toronja; *Arg.* pomelo (toh-ROHN-hah; poh-MAY-loh)

gravy n. salsa (SAHL-sah)

gray n., adj. gris (grees)

great adj. gran; grande (grahn; GRAHN-day)

great deal adj., adv. mucho (MOO-choh)

green n., adj. verde (VAHR-day)

greet v. saludar (sah-loo-DAHR)

greeting n. saludo (sah-LOO-doh)

grocery n. *Cuba, PR, Ven.* bodega; *Mex.* abarrotes (boh-DAY-gah; ah-bah-ROH-tays)

ground floor n. piso bajo; *Mex.* planta baja (PEE-soh BAH-hoh; PLAHN-tah BAH-hah)

group n. grupo (GROO-poh)

guarantee v. garantizar (gah-rahn-tee-SAHR)

guaranty n. garantía (gah-rahn-TEE-ah)

guest n. invitado (een-vee-TAH-doh)

guide n. guía (GHEE-ah)

guidebook n. guía (GHEE-ah)

guitar n. guitarra (ghee-TAH-rah)

gulf n. golfo (GOHL-foh)

gum n. goma; chicle (GOH-mah; CHEE-clay)

gun n. fusil (foo-SEEL)

gymnasium n. gimnasio (heem-NAH-see-oh)

H

hair n. pelo (PAY-loh)

hairdresser n. peluquero (pay-loo-KAY-roh)

half adj. medio (MAY-dee-oh)

hall n. pasillo (pah-SEE-yoh)

ham n. jamón (hah-MOHN)

hamburger n. hamburguesa (ahm-boor-GAY-sah)

hand n. mano (MAH-noh)

handbag n. cartera; *Ec.* bolso; *Mex.* bolsa (cahr-TAY-rah; BOHL-soh; BOHL-sah)

handle n. manija (mah-NEE-hah)

handrail n. pasamanos (pah-sah-MAH-nohs)

handsome adj. guapo; bello; *Uru.* bien parecido (GWAH-poh; BAY-yoh; bee-AYN pah-ray-SEE-doh)

hanger n. colgador; *Mex.* gancho; *Cuba* perchero (cohl-gah-DOHR; GAHN-choh; payr-CHAY-roh)

happen v. pasar (pah-SAHR)

happy adj. feliz (fay-LEES)

hard adj. duro; difícil (DOO-roh; dee-FEE-seel)

hardware store n. ferretería (fay-ray-tay-REE-ah)

harm n. daño; v. dañar (DAH-nyoh; dah-NYAHR)

hat n. sombrero (sohm-BRAY-roh)

hate n. odio; v. odiar (OH-dee-oh; oh-dee-AHR)

have v. tener (tay-NAYR)

have fun v. divertir(se) (dee-vayr-TEER-say)

he pron. él (ayl)

head n. cabeza (cah-BAY-sah)

headache n. dolor de cabeza (doh-LOHR de cah-BAY-sah)

health n. salud (sah-LOOD)

healthy adj. saludable; sano (sah-loo-DAH-blay; SAH-noh)

hear v. oír; escuchar (oh-EER; ess-coo-CHAHR)

heart n. corazón (coh-rah-SOHN)

heat n. calor (cah-LOHR)

heaven n. cielo (see-AY-loh)

heavy adj. pesado (pay-SAH-doh)

heel n. tacón (shoe) (tah-COHN)

height n. altura (ahl-TOO-rah)

Help! interj. ¡Socorro! (soh-COH-roh)

here adv. aquí (ah-KEY)

hide v. esconder (ess-cohn-DAYR)

highway n. carretera (cah-ray-TAY-rah)

hire v. alquilar (ahl-key-LAHR)

hole n. agujero; hueco (ah-goo-HAY-roh; WAY-coh)

holiday n. día festivo (DEE-ah fays-TEE-voh)

home n. hogar; adv. a casa; en casa (oh-GAHR; ah CAH-sah; ayn CAH-sah)

homeland n. patria (PAH-tree-ah)

honest adj. honesto (oh-NAYS-toh)

honeymoon n. luna de miel (LOO-nah day mee-AYL)

hope n. esperanza; v. esperar (ess-pay-RAHN-sah; ess-pay-RAHR)

hors d'oeuvres n. entremeses; *Mex.* botanas (ayn-tray-MAY-says; boh-TAH-nahs)

horse n. caballo (cah-BAH-yoh)

hospital n. hospital (ohs-pee-TAHL)

hot adj. caliente; picante (spicy) (cah-lee-AYN-tay; pee-CAHN-tay)

hot-dog n. perro caliente (PAY-roh cah-lee-AYN-tay)

hotel n. hotel (oh-TAYL)

hour n. hora (OH-rah)

house n. casa (CAH-sah)

how adv. como (COH-moh)

however conj. sin embargo (seen aym-BAHR-goh)

how many? ¿cuántos? (KWAN-tohs)

how much? ¿cuánto? (KWAN-toh)

how soon? ¿cuándo? (KWAN-doh)

hundred n., adj. cien; ciento (see-AYN; see-AYN-toh)

hunger n. hambre (AHM-bray)

hunt v. cazar (cah-SAHR)

hurry v. ir de prisa (eer day PREE-sah)

husband n. esposo; marido (ess-POH-soh; mah-REE-doh)

I

I pron. yo (yoh)

ice n. hielo (ee-AY-loh)

ice cream n. helado; *PR* mantecado (ay-LAH-doh; mahn-tay-CAH-doh)

idea n. idea (ee-DAY-ah)

identity card n. cédula (de identidad) (SAY-doo-lah de ee-dayn-tee-TAHD)

if conj. si (see)

ill adj. enfermo (ayn-FAYR-moh)

illegal adj. ilegal (ee-lay-GAHL)

image n. imagen (ee-MAH-hen)

imagine v. imaginar (ee-mah-hee-NAHR)

immediately adv. en seguida; *Mex.* ahorita (ayn say-GHEE-dah; ah-oh-REE-tah)

immigrant n. inmigrante (een-mee-GRAHN-tay)

import v. importar (eem-pohr-TAHR)

importance n. importancia (eem-pohr-TAHN-see-ah)

important adj. importante (eem-pohr-TAHN-tay)

importer n. importador (eem-pohr-tah-DOHR)

imports n. importaciones (eem-pohr-tah-see-OH-nays)

impossible adj. imposible (eem-pohs-SEE-blay)

impress v. impresionar (eem-pray-see-oh-NAHR)

impressive adj. impresionante (eem-pray-see-oh-NAHN-tay)

improve v. mejorar (may-hoh-RAHR)

in prep. en (ayn)

in advance adv. por adelantado (pohr ah-day-lahn-TAH-doh)

in case conj. en caso (ayn CAH-soh)

inch n. pulgada (pool-GAH-dah)

include v. incluir (een-cloo-EER)

including prep. incluso (een-CLOO-soh)

income n. ingreso (een-GRAY-soh)

income tax n. impuesto de utilidades (eem-PWAYS-toh day oo-tee-lee-DAH-days)

increase v. aumentar (ay-oo-mayn-TAHR)

independent adj. independiente (een-day-payn-dee-AYN-tay)

indicate v. indicar (een-dee-CAHR)

industry n. industria (een-DOOS-tree-ah)

inexpensive adj. barato (bah-RAH-toh)

inferior adj. inferior (een-fay-ree-OHR)

inside adv. adentro (ah-DAYN-troh)

insist v. insistir (een-see-STEER)

inspect v. inspeccionar (een-spayk-see-oh-NAHR)

instead of prep. en vez de (ayn vays day)

institute n. instituto (een-stee-TOO-toh)

instruction n. instrucción (een-strook-see-OHN)

insult v. insultar (een-sool-TAHR)

insurance n. seguro (say-GOO-roh)

insure v. asegurar (ay-say-goo-RAHR)

intelligent adj. inteligente (een-tay-lee-HAYN-tay)

intercity bus n. *Arg.* micro; *Carib.*, *Mex.* autobús; *Pe.*, *Uru.* ómnibus (MEE-croh; ah-oo-toh-BOOS; OHM-nee-boos)

interpreter n. intérprete (een-TAYR-pray-tay)

into prep. en; adentro (ayn; ah-DAYN-troh)

introduce v. presentar (pray-sayn-TAHR)

invitation n. invitación (een-vee-tah-see-OHN)

invite v. invitar (een-vee-TAHR)

iron n. plancha; v. planchar (PLAHN-chah; plahn-CHAHR)

island n. isla (EES-lah)

item n. artículo (ahr-TEE-coo-loh)

J

jacket n. chaqueta; *Mex.* chamarra; *Pe.* casaca (chah-
    KAY-tah; chah-MAH-rah; cah-SAH-cah)

jail n. cárcel (CAHR-sayl)

jam n. mermelada (mayr-may-LAH-dah)

January n. enero (ay-NAY-roh)

jellyfish n. *Bol., Uru.* medusa; *Cuba, Mex.* aguamala
    (may-DOO-sah; ah-gwah-MAH-lah)

jewel n. joya (HOH-yah)

jewelry n. joyería (hoh-yay-REE-ah)

job n. empleo (aym-PLAY-oh)

joke n. broma; chiste (BROH-mah; CHEES-tay)

juice n. jugo; *CR* zumo (HOO-goh; SOO-moh)

July n. julio (HOO-lee-oh)

jump v. saltar; *Mex.* brincar (sahl-TAHR; breen-CAHR)

jungle n. selva (SAYL-vah)

June n. junio (HOO-nee-oh)

justice n. justicia (hoos-TEE-see-ah)

K

keep v. mantener (mahn-tay-NAYR)

key n. llave (YAH-vay)

kid n. *Cuba, Pe.* chico; *Mex.* chamaco (CHEE-coh;
    chah-MAH-coh)

kill v. matar (mah-TAHR)

kilogram n. kilo(gramo) (key-loh-GRAH-moh)

kilometer n. kilómetro (key-LOH-may-troh)

kind adj. bondadoso (bohn-dah-DOH-soh)

kiss n. beso; v. besar (BAY-soh; bay-SAHR)

kitchen n. cocina (coh-SEE-nah)

knee n. rodilla (roh-DEE-yah)

knife n. cuchillo (coo-CHEE-yoh)

knock v. tocar (toh-CAHR)

know v. saber; conocer (sah-BAYR; coh-noh-SAYR)

know how v. saber (say-BAYR)

knowledge n. conocimiento (coh-noh-see-mee-
    AYN-toh)

L

label n. etiqueta (ay-tee-KAY-tah)

lace n. encaje (ayn-CAH-hay)

lack n. falta; v. faltar (FAHL-tah; fahl-TAHR)

lady n. señora; dama (say-NYOHR-ah; DAH-mah)

lake n. lago (LAH-goh)

lamp n. lámpara (LAHM-pah-rah)

land n. tierra; v. aterrizar (tee-AY-rah; ah-tay-ree-
    SAHR)

landscape n. paisaje (pah-ee-SAH-hay)

language n. idioma (ee-dee-OH-mah)

large adj. grande (GRAHN-day)

last adj. ultimo (OOL-tee-moh)

last name n. apellido (ah-pay-YEE-doh)

late adv. tarde (TAHR-day)

laugh n. risa; v. reír(se) (REE-sah; ray-EER-say)

laundry n. lavandería (lah-vahn-day-REE-ah)

law n. ley (lay)

lawyer n. abogado; *Mex.* licenciado (ah-boh-GAH-doh; lee-sayn-see-AH-doh)

lazy adj. flojo; *Cuba* vago (FLOH-hoh; VAH-goh)

leader n. dirigente (dee-ree-HAYN-tay)

learn v. aprender (ah-prayn-DAYR)

least adj. menor (may-NOHR)

leather n. cuero (coo-AY-roh)

leave v. salir (sah-LEER)

leave out v. omitir (oh-mee-TEER)

left adj. izquierdo (ees-key-AHR-doh)

leg n. pierna (pee-AYR-nah)

legal adj. legal (lay-GAHL)

lemon n. limón (lee-MOHN)

lemonade n. limonada (lee-moh-NAH-dah)

lend v. prestar (prays-TAHR)

length n. largo (LAHR-goh)

lens n. lente (LAYN-tay)

less adj., adv. menos (MAY-nohs)

letter n. carta (CAHR-tah)

lettuce n. lechuga (lay-CHOO-gah)

library n. biblioteca (bee-blee-oh-TAY-cah)

license (driver's) n. *Arg.* permiso de manejo; *Mex.*
   licencia (de conducir) (payr-MEE-soh day mah-
   NAY-hoh; lee-SAYN-see-ah day cohn-doo-SEER)

lie n. mentira (mayn-TEE-rah)

life n. vida (VEE-dah)

life insurance n. seguro de vida (say-GOO-roh day
   VEE-dah)

lift v. levantar (lay-vahn-TAHR)

light n. luz (loos)

light bulb n. bombilla; *Arg.* lamparita; *Mex.* foco
   (bohm-BEE-yah; lahm-pah-REE-tah; FOH-coh)

like v. gustar (goos-TAHR)

lime n. limón (lee-MOHN)

liquor n. licor (lee-COHR)

list n. lista (LEES-tah)

listen v. escuchar (ess-coo-CHAHR)

little adj., adv. poco; pequeño; chico (POH-coh; pay-
   KAY-nyoh; CHEE-coh)

live v. vivir (vee-VEEHR)

living room n. sala (SAH-lah)

lobster n. langosta (lahn-GHOHS-tah)

long adj. largo (LAHR-goh)

look at v. mirar (mee-RAHR)

look for v. buscar (boos-CAHR)

lose v. perder (payr-DAYHR)

lottery n. lotería (loh-tay-REE-ah)

loud adj. alto; fuerte (AHL-toh; FWAR-tay)

love n. amor; v. amar; querer (ah-MOHR; ah-MAHR; kay-RAYR)

luck n. suerte (SWAYR-tay)

luggage n. equipaje (ay-key-PAH-hay)

lunch (midday meal) n. *Bol., Cuba, Ven.* almuerzo, *Mex.* comida (ahl-moo-AYR-soh; coh-MEE-dah)

luxury n. lujo (LOO-hoh)

M

machine n. máquina (MAH-key-nah)

magazine n. revista (ray-VEES-tah)

maid n. criada; *Bol., Ec., Pan.* empleada; *Mex., Uru.* sirvienta (cree-AH-dah; aym-play-AH-dah; seer-vee-AYN-tah)

mail n. correo; v. echar al correo (coh-RAY-oh; ay-CHAHR ahl coh-RAY-oh)

main adj. principal (preen-see-PAHL)

main square n. plaza mayor; *Mex.* zócalo (PLAH-sah mah-YOHR; SOH-cah-loh)

make v. hacer (ah-SAYR)

make a mistake v. equivocar(se) (ay-key-voh-CAHR-say)

man n. hombre (OHM-bray)

manager n. gerente (hay-RAHN-tay)

many adj. muchos (MOO-chohs)

map n. mapa (MAH-pah)

March n. marzo (MAHR-soh)

market n. mercado (mayr-CAH-doh)

married adj. casado (cah-SAH-doh)

match n. fósforo; *Mex.* cerillo (FOHS-foh-roh; say-REE-yoh)

May n. mayo (MAH-yoh)

me pron. me; a mí (may; ah mee)

meal n. comida (coh-MEE-dah)

meat n. carne (CAHR-nay)

meet v. conocer; encontrar (coh-noh-SAYR; ayn-cohn-TRAHR)

meeting n. reunión (ray-oo-nee-OHN)

melon n. melón (may-LOHN)

merchandise n. mercancía (mayr-cahn-SEE-ah)

139

message n. recado (ray-CAH-doh)

meter n. metro (MAY-troh)

mile n. milla (MEE-yah)

milk n. leche (LAY-chay)

million n. millón (mee-YOHN)

minute n. minuto (mee-NOO-toh)

Miss n. señorita (say-nyohr-REE-tah)

mistake n. error (ay-ROHR)

moment n. momento (moh-MAYN-toh)

Monday n. lunes (LOO-nays)

money n. dinero (dee-NAY-roh)

money order n. giro; *Ven.* orden de pago (HEE-roh;
    OHR-dayn day PAH-goh)

month n. mes (mays)

more adj., adv. más (mahs)

morning n. mañana (mah-NYAH-nah)

mosquito n. mosquito (mohs-KEY-toh)

most n. la major parte (de) (lah mah-YOHR PAHR-
    tay day)

mother n. madre; *Mex.* mamá (MAH-dray; mah-
    MAH)

motor n. motor (moh-TOHR)

motorcycle n. motocicleta (moh-toh-see-CLAY-tah)

mountain n. montaña (mohn-TAH-nyah)

mouth n. boca (BOH-cah)

Mr. n. señor (say-NYOR)

Mrs. n. señora (say-NYOH-rah)

much adj., adv. mucho (MOO-choh)

museum n. museo (moo-SAY-oh)

music n. música (MOO-see-cah)

must v. tener que (tay-NAHR kay)

my adj. mi; mío (mee; MEE-oh)

N

name n. nombre (NOHM-bray)

nap n. siesta (see-AYS-tah)

napkin n. servilleta (sayr-vee-YAY-tah)

nation n. nación (nah-see-OHN)

national adj. nacional (nah-see-oh-NAHL)

near adv. cerca; prep. cerca de (SAYR-cah day)

necessary adj. necesario (nay-say-SAHR-ee-oh)

neck n. cuello (coo-AY-yoh)

need v. necesitar (nay-say-see-TAHR)

neither adj. ninguno; conj. ni (neen-GOO-noh; nee)

never adv. nunca (NOON-cah)

nevertheless adv. sin embargo (seen aym-BAHR-goh)

new adj. nuevo (noo-AY-voh)

news n. noticias (noh-TEE-see-ahs)

newspaper n. periódico (pay-ree-OH-dee-coh)

next adj. próximo (PROCK-see-moh)

nice adj. simpático (seem-PAH-tee-coh)

night n. noche (NOH-chay)

nine n., adj. nueve (noo-AY-vay)

nineteen n., adj. diez y nueve (dee-AYS ee noo-AY-vay)

ninety n., adj. noventa (noh-VAYN-tah)

no adj. ninguno; adv. no (neen-GOO-noh; noh)

nobody pron. nadie (NAH-dee-ay)

noise n. ruido (roo-EE-doh)

noon n. mediodía (may-dee-oh-DEE-ah)

nor conj. ni (nee)

north n. norte (NOHR-tay)

nose n. nariz (nahr-EES)

note n. nota; v. notar (NOH-tah; noh-TAHR)

nothing pron. nada (NAH-dah)

November n. noviembre (noh-vee-AYM-bray)

now adv. ahora (ah-OH-rah)

number n. número (NOO-may-roh)

nurse n. enfermera (ayn-fayr-MAY-rah)

O

observe v. observar (ohb-sayr-VAHR)

obtain v. obtener (ohb-tay-NAYR)

occasionally adv. de vez en cuando (day vays ayn KWAN-doh)

occupation n. ocupación (oh-coo-pah-see-OHN)

occupy v. ocupar (oh-coo-PAHR)

occur v. ocurrir (oh-coo-REER)

October n. octubre (ok-TOO-bray)

of prep. de (day)

offer n. ofrecimiento; ofrecer (oh-fray-see-mee-AYN-toh; oh-fray-SAYR)

office n. oficina; *Arg., Ec., Pe.* (leg.); *Mex.* (leg.) bufete; (med.) consultorio (oh-fee-SEE-nah; boo-FAY-tay; cohn-sool-TOH-ree-oh)

officer n. oficial (oh-fee-see-AHL)

official n., adj. oficial (oh-fee-see-AHL)

often adv. frecuentemente (fray-kwayn-tay-MAYN-tay)

oil n. aceite (ah-SAY-tay)

old adj. viejo (vee-AY-hoh)

olive n. aceituna (ah-say-TOO-nah)

omelet n. *Cuba* tortilla (tohr-TEE-yah)

omit v. omitir (oh-mee-TEER)

on prep. en; sobre (ayn; SOH-bray)

once adv. una vez (OO-nah vays)

once more adv. otra vez (OH-trah vays)

one adj. un; una (oon; OO-nah)

onion n. cebolla (say-BOH-yah)

only adj. sólo; adv. solamente (SOH-loh; soh-lah-
    MAYN-tay)

open adj. abierto; v. abrir (ah-bee-AYR-toh; ah-BREER)

opportunity n. oportunidad (oh-pohr-too-nee-DAHD)

or conj. o (oh)

orange n. naranja (nah-RAHN-hah)

orange juice n. jugo de naranja; *PR* jugo de china
    (HOO-goh day nah-RAHN-hah; HOO-goh day
    CHEE-nah)

order n. orden; v. pedir (OHR-dayn; pay-DEER)

organization n. organización (ohr-gah-nee-sah-
    see-OHN)

organize v. organizar (ohr-gah-nee-SAHR)

other adj., pron. otro (OH-troh)

ounce n. onza (OHN-sah)

our adj. nuestro (noo-AYS-troh)

out adv. fuera (FWAY-rah)

outlet n. (elect.) toma-corriente; *Mex.* contacto (TOH-
    mah coh-ree-AYN-tay; cohn-TAYK-toh)

over prep. sobre (SOH-bray)

overweight n. sobrepeso (soh-bray-PAY-soh)

owe v. deber (day-BAYR)

owner n. dueño (doo-AY-nyoh)

P

package n. paquete (pah-KAY-tay)

page n. página (PAH-hee-nah)

pain n. dolor (doh-LOHR)

painter n. pintor (peen-TOHR)

pair n. pareja (couple); par (pah-RAY-hah; pahr)

pajamas n. pijamas (pee-CHAH-mahs)

pants n. pantalones; *Mex.* pantalón (pahn-tah-LOH-nays; pahn-tah-LOHN)

paper n. papel (pah-PAYL)

pardon n. perdón (payr-DOHN)

park n. parque; v. estacionar, *Cuba* parquear (PAHR-kay; ess-tah-see-oh-NAHR; pahr-kay-AHR)

parking n. estacionamiento; *Bol., Cuba* parqueo (ays-tah-see-oh-nah-mee-AYN-toh; pahr-KAY-oh)

part n. parte (PAHR-tay)

participate v. participar (pahr-tee-see-PAHR)

party n. fiesta; (pol.) partido (fee-AYS-tah)

pass n. pase; v. pasar (PAH-say; pah-SAHR)

passenger n. pasajero (pah-sah-HAY-roh)

passport n. pasaporte (pah-sah-POHR-tay)

past n., adj. pasado (pah-SAH-doh)

pay v. pagar (pay-GAHR)

payment n. pago (PAH-goh)

peach n. melocotón; *Arg., Mex., Pan.* durazno (may-loh-coh-TOHN; doo-RAHS-noh)

peak n. pico; (PEE-coh)

peanut n. maní; *Mex.* cacahuate (mah-NEE; cah-cah-oo-AH-tay)

pearl n. perla (PAYR-lah)

peasant n. campesino; *Cuba* guajiro; *PR* jíbaro (cahm-pay-SEE-noh; gwah-HEE-roh; HEE-bah-roh)

pedestrian n. peatón (pay-ah-TOHN)

pen n. pluma (PLOO-mah)

pencil n. lápiz (LAH-pees)

penny n. centavo (sayn-TAH-voh)

people n. gente (HAYN-tay)

pepper n. pimienta (pee-mee-AYN-tah)

per prep. por (pohr)

percent n., adj. por ciento (pohr see-AYN-toh)

percentage n. porcentaje (pohr-sayn-TAH-hay)

performance n. función (foon-see-OHN)

perfume n. perfume (payr-FOO-may)

perhaps adv. quizás (key-SAHS)

permission n. permiso (payr-MEE-soh)

permit v. permitir (payr-mee-TEER)

person n. persona (payr-SOH-nah)

petroleum n. petróleo (pay-TROH-lay-oh)

photograph n. foto; v. sacar foto (FOH-toh; sah-CAHR FOH-toh)

picture n. cuadro (KWAH-droh)

pie n. *Arg.* torta; *Cuba* pastel; *Mex.* pay (TOHR-tah; PAHS-tayl; pay)

pillow n. almohada (ahl-moh-AH-dah)

pineapple n. piña; *Arg.* ananá (PEE-nyah; ah-nah-NAH)

pink adj. rosado (roh-SAH-doh)

place n. lugar; v. poner (loo-GAHR; poh-NAYR)

plane n. avión (ah-vee-OHN)

plant n. planta; v. plantar (PLAHN-tah; plahn-TAHR)

plate n. plato (PLAH-toh)

play n. drama; v. jugar (DRAH-mah; hoo-GAHR)

police n. policía; *Arg.* botón (poh-lee-SEE-ah; boh-TOHN)

pool n. piscina; *Mex.* alberca (pee-SEE-nah; ahl-BAYR-cah)

poor adj. pobre (POH-bray)

pop n. refresco; gaseosa (ray-FRAYS-coh; gah-say-OH-sah)

popcorn n. *Bol.* pipocas; *Cuba* rositas de maíz; *Mex.* palomitas (pee-POH-cahs; roh-SEE-tahs day mah-EES; pah-loh-MEE-tahs)

pork n. carne de puerco (CAHR-nay day PWAYR-coh)

port n. puerto (PWAYR-toh)

position n. posición (poh-see-see-OHN)

possible adj. posible (poh-SEE-blay)

postcard n. tarjeta postal (tahr-HAY-tah pohs-TAHL)

post office n. casa de correos; *Mex.* oficina de correos
(CAH-sah day coh-RAY-ohs; oh-fee-SEE-nah day
coh-RAY-ohs)

potato n. papa (PAH-pah)

pound n. libra (LEE-brah)

power n. poder (poh-DAYR)

practice v. practicar (prak-tee-CAHR)

prefer v. preferir (pray-fay-REER)

prepare v. preparar (pray-pah-RAHR)

prescription n. (med.) receta (ray-SAY-tah)

present v. presentar (pray-sayn-TAHR)

president n. presidente (pray-see-DAYN-tay)

pretty adj. bonito (boh-NEE-toh)

price n. precio (PRAY-see-oh)

priest n. cura (COO-rah)

printer n. impresor (eem-pray-SOHR)

prison n. prisión (pree-see-OHN)

private adj. privado (pree-VAH-doh)

probable adj. probable (proh-BAH-blay)

problem n. problema (proh-BLAY-mah)

produce v. producir (proh-doo-SEER)

product n. producto (proh-DOOK-toh)

prohibit v. prohibir (proh-ee-BEER)

promise v. prometer (proh-may-TAYR)

prostitute n. prostituta (prohs-tee-TOO-tah)

protection n. protección (proh-tayk-see-OHN)

public n., adj. público (POO-blee-coh)

pull v. tirar; jalar (tee-RAHR; hah-LAHR)

punctual adj. puntual (poon-too-AHL)

pure adj. puro (POO-roh)

purple n., adj. morado (moh-RAH-doh)

purpose n. propósito (proh-POH-see-toh)

purse n. bolsa (BOHL-sah)

push v. empujar (aym-poo-HAHR)

put v. poner (poh-NAYR)

put on v. poner(se) (poh-NAYR-say)

pyramid n. pirámide (pee-RAH-mee-day)

Q

quality n. calidad (cah-lee-DAHD)

quantity n. cantidad (cahn-tee-DAHD)

question n. pregunta; v. preguntar (pray-GOON-tah; pray-goon-TAHR)

quiet adj. tranquilo (trahn-KEY-loh)

quite adv. bastante (bahs-TAHN-tay)

R

radio n. radio (RAH-dee-oh)

railway n. ferrocarril (fay-roh-cah-REEL)

rain n. lluvia; v. llover (YOO-vee-ah; yoh-VAYR)

raincoat n. impermeable (eem-payr-may-AH-blay)

raise v. levantar (lay-vayn-TAHR)

rapid adj. rápido (RAH-pee-doh)

rare adj. medio crudo (MAY-dee-oh CROO-doh)

rate n. tarifa (tah-REE-fah)

rate of exchange n. tipo de cambio (TEE-poh day CAHM-bee-oh)

razor n. máquina de afeitar (MAH-key-NAH day ah-fay-TAHR)

razor blade n. hoja de afeitar; *Mex.* hoja de rasurar (OH-hah day ah-fay-TAHR; OH-hah day rah-soo-RAHR)

read v. leer (lay-AYR)

ready adj. listo (LEES-toh)

real adj. verdadero (vayr-dah-DAY-roh)

realize v. dar(se) cuenta de (dahr-say coo-AYN-tah day)

receipt n. recibo (ray-SEE-boh)

receive v. recibir (ray-see-VEER)

recent adj. reciente (ray-see-AYN-tay)

recognize v. reconocer (ray-coh-noh-SAYR)

recommend v. recomendar (ray-coh-mayn-DAHR)

red n., adj. rojo (ROH-hoh)

refer v. referir (ray-fay-REER)

refuse v. rehusar (ray-oo-SAHR)

register n. registro (ray-HEES-troh)

rely v. confiar (cohn-fee-AHR)

remain v. quedar(se) (kay-DAHR-say)

remember v. recordar (ray-cohr-DAHR)

remit v. remitir (ray-mee-TEER)

repeat v. repetir (ray-pay-TEER)

reply n. respuesta; v. responder (rays-PWAYS-tah; rays-pohn-DAYR)

report n. informe; v. informar (een-FOHR-may; een-fohr-MAHR)

request v. pedir (pay-DEER)

reservation n. reservación (ray-sayr-vah-see-OHN)

reserve v. reservar (ray-sayr-VAHR)

responsible adj. responsable (rays-pohn-SAH-blay)

rest v. descansar (days-cahn-SAHR)

restaurant n. restaurante (rays-tah-oo-RAHN-tay)

retail n. venta al menudeo (VAYN-tah ahl may-noo-DAY-oh)

return v. regresar; volver (ray-gray-SAHR; vohl-VAYR)

rice n. arroz (ah-ROHS)

rich adj. rico (REE-coh)

right n. derecho; adj. correcto; derecho (direction) (day-RAY-choh; coh-RAYK-toh)

right now adv. ahora mismo; *Ec.*, *Mex.* ahorita (ah-OH-rah MEES-moh; ah-oh-REE-tah)

right there adv. allí mismo (ah-EE MEES-moh)

river n. río (REE-oh)

road n. camino (cah-MEE-noh)

roast n. asado (ah-SAH-doh)

rob v. robar (roh-BAHR)

robber n. ladrón (lah-DROHN)

room n. cuarto; habitación; *Arg.*, *Chi.* pieza (KWAHR-toh; ah-bee-tah-see-OHN; pee-AY-sah)

route n. ruta (ROO-tah)

rubbish n. basura (bah-SOO-rah)

ruby n. rubí (roo-BEE)

rug n. alfombra; *Mex.* tapete (ahl-FOHM-brah; tah-PAY-tay)

rum n. ron (rohn)

run v. correr (coh-RAYR)

rush v. ir de prisa (eer day PREE-sah)

S

sad adj. triste (TREES-tay)

safe n. caja de seguridad; adj. seguro (CAH-hah day say-goo-ree-DAHD; say-GOO-roh)

safety n. seguridad (say-goo-ree-DAHD)

salad n. ensalada (ayn-sah-LAH-dah)

salary n. salario (sah-LAH-ree-oh)

sale n. venta; *Mex.* barata (VAYN-tah; bah-RAH-tah)

salt n. sal (sahl)

same adj. mismo (MEES-moh)

sample n. muestra (moo-AYS-trah)

sandwich n. sandwich; emparedado; *Cuba* bocadito; *Ec.* sánduche (SAHN-doo-eech; aym-pah-ray-DAH-doh; boh-cah-DEE-toh; SAHN-doo-chay)

satisfactory adj. satisfactorio (sah-tees-fahk-TOH-ree-oh)

Saturday n. sábado (SAH-bah-doh)

sauce n. salsa (SAHL-sah)

sausage n. salchicha (frankfurter) (sahl-CHEE-chah)

save v. salvar; ahorrar (money) (sahl-VAHR; ah-oh-RAHR)

say v. decir (day-SEER)

schedule n. horario (oh-RAH-ree-oh)

school n. escuela (ess-KWAY-lah)

scissors n. tijeras (tee-HAY-rahs)

sculptor n. escultor (ays-cool-TOHR)

sea n. mar (mahr)

season n. estación (ess-tah-see-OHN)

seat n. asiento; v. sentar (ah-see-AYN-toh; sayn-TAHR)

secretary n. secretario/a (say-cray-TAH-ree-oh/ah)

security n. seguridad (say-goo-ree-DAHD)

see v. ver (vayr)

seek v. buscar (boos-CAHR)

seem v. parecer (pah-ray-SAYR)

sell v. vender (vayn-DAYR)

send v. enviar (ayn-vee-AHR)

separate adj. separado (say-pah-RAH-doh)

separate v. separar (say-pah-RAHR)

separation n. separacion (say-pah-rah-see-OHN)

September n. septiembre (sayp-tee-AYM-bray)

servant n. criado; sirviente (cree-AH-doh; seer-vee-AYN-tay)

service n. servicio (sayr-VEE-see-oh)

seven n., adj. siete (see-AY-tay)

seventy n., adj. setenta (say-TAYN-tah)

several adj. varios (VAH-ree-ohs)

shampoo n. champú (chahm-POO)

share n. (com.) acción; v. compartir (ahk-see-OHN; cohm-pahr-TEER)

shareholder n. (com.) accionista (ahk-see-ohn-NEES-tah)

shark n. tiburón (tee-BOO-rohn)

sharp adj. agudo (ah-GOO-doh)

shave v. afeitar(se); *CA, Mex.* rasurar(se) (ah-fay-TAHR-say; rah-soo-RAHR-say)

she pron. ella (AY-yah)

sheet n. hoja (paper); sábana (bed) (OH-hah; SAH-bah-nah)

shellfish n. mariscos (mah-REES-cohs)

sherry n. vino de jerez (VEE-noh day hay-RAYS)

shirt n. camisa (cah-MEE-sah)

shoe n. zapato (sah-PAH-toh)

shoeshine boy n. limpiabotas; *Mex.* bolero (leem-pee-ah-BOH-tahs; boh-LAY-roh)

shop n. tienda; v. ir de compras (tee-AYN-dah; eer day COHM-prahs)

short adj. corto; bajo (stature) (COHR-toh; BAH-hoh)

shout v. gritar (gree-TAHR)

show v. mostrar (mohs-TRAHR)

shower n. *Carib.* ducha; *Mex.* regadera (DOO-chah; ray-gah-DAY-rah)

shrimp n. camarones (cah-mah-ROHN-ays)

sick adj. malo; enfermo (MAH-loh; ayn-FAYR-moh)

sidewalk n. acera; *Arg., CA, Mex.* banqueta (ah-SAY-rah; bahn-KAY-tah)

sign v. firmar (feer-MAHR)

signature n. firma (FEER-mah)

silk n. seda (SAY-dah)

silver n. plata (PLAH-tah)

simple adj. sencillo (sayn-SEE-yoh)

since adv. desde (DAYS-day)

sing v. cantar (cahn-TAHR)

singer n. cantante (cahn-TAHN-tay)

sister n. hermana (ayr-MAH-nah)

sit down v. sentar(se) (sayn-TAHR-say)

six n., adj. seis (says)

sixty n., adj. sesenta (say-SAYN-tah)

size n. tamaño (tah-MAH-nyoh)

skin n. piel (pee-AYL)

skirt n. falda; *Cuba* saya (FAHL-dah; SAH-yah)

sleep n. sueño; v. dormir (SWAY-nyo; dohr-MEER)

sleeve n. manga (MAHN-gah)

slow adj. lento (LAYN-toh)

slowly adv. despacio (days-PAH-see-oh)

small adj. pequeño; chico (pay-KAY-nyoh; CHEE-coh)

smart adj. inteligente (een-tay-lee-HAYN-tay)

smoke v. fumar (foo-MAHR)

snack n. merienda; *Chi.* las onces; *Mex.* botanas (may-ree-AYN-dah; lahs OHN-says; boh-TAH-nahs)

soap n. jabón (hah-BOHN)

soccer n. fútbol; balompié (FOOT-bohl; bah-lohm-
  pee-AY)

society n. sociedad (soh-see-ay-DAHD)

sock n. calcetín; media (cahl-say-TEEN; MAY-dee-ah)

soft drink n. refresco; *Pe.* gaseosa (ray-FRAYS-coh;
  gah-say-OH-sah)

sole n. suela (shoe) (SWAY-lah)

solve v. resolver (ray-sohl-VAYR)

some adj. algunos; unos (ahl-GOO-nohs; OO-nohs)

somebody n., pron. alguien (AHL-ghee-ayn)

something n., pron. algo (AHL-goh)

sometimes adv. a veces (ah VAY-says)

son n. hijo (EE-hoh)

song n. canción (cahn-see-OHN)

soon adv. pronto (PROHN-toh)

soup n. sopa (SOH-pah)

south n. sur (soor)

souvenir n. recuerdo (ray-KWAYR-doh)

speak v. hablar (ah-BLAHR)

special adj. especial (ess-pay-see-AHL)

speech n. discurso (dees-COOR-soh)

spend v. gastar (gah-STAHR)

spicy adj. picante (pee-CAHN-tay)

spinach n. espinacas (ess-pee-NAH-cahs)

spoon n. cuchara (coo-CHAH-rah)

sport n. deporte (day-POHR-tay)

spring n. primavera (pree-mah-VAYR-ah)

staff n. personal (payr-soh-NAHL)

stairs n. escalera (ess-cah-LAY-rah)

stamp n. estampilla; *Arg., Cuba* sello; *Mex.* timbre
(ess-tahm-PEE-yah; SAY-yoh; TEEM-bray)

start v. comenzar; empezar (coh-mayn-SAHR; aym-
pay-SAHR)

state n. estado (ess-TAH-doh)

statement n. declaración; (com.) estado de cuenta
(day-clah-rah-see-OHN; ess-TAH-doh day coo-
AYN-tah)

station n. estación (ess-tah-see-OHN)

stationery store n. papelería (pah-pay-lay-REE-ah)

statue n. estatua (ess-TAH-too-ah)

stay v. quedar(se) (kay-DAHR-say)

steak n. biftec; *RP* bife (beef-TAYK; BEE-fay)

steal v. robar (roh-BAHR)

stew n. *Mex.* guisado *RP* guiso (ghee-SAH-doh;
GHEE-soh)

still adv. todavía (toh-dah-VEE-ah)

stockbroker n. corredor de bolsa (coh-ray-DOHR day
BOHL-sah)

stock exchange n. bolsa (BOHL-sah)

stockings n. medias (MAY-dee-ahs)

stomach n. estómago (ess-TOH-mah-goh)

stomachache n. dolor de estómago (doh-LOHR day
    ess-TOH-mah-goh)

stop n. parada; v. detener (pah-RAH-dah; day-tayn-AYR)

store n. tienda (tee-AYN-dah)

straight adj., adv. derecho (day-RAY-choh)

straw (drinking) n. *Bol.* bombilla; *Chi.*, *Uru.* pajita;
    Mex. popote (bohm-BEE-yah; pah-HEE-tah;
    poh-POH-tay)

strawberry n. fresa (FRAY-sah)

street n. calle (CAH-yay)

strong adj. fuerte (FWAYR-tay)

struggle n. lucha; v. luchar (LOO-chah; loo-CHAHR)

student n. estudiante (ess-too-dee-AHN-tay)

study v. estudiar (ess-too-dee-AHR)

subway n. subterráneo; *Mex.* metro (soob-tay-RAH-
    nay-oh; MAY-troh)

success n. éxito (EX-ee-toh)

such adj., pron. tal (tahl)

suddenly adv. de repente (de ray-PAYN-tay)

sugar n. azúcar (ah-SOO-cahr)

suit n. traje (TRAH-hay)

summer n. verano (vay-RAH-noh)

sun n. sol (sohl)

Sunday n. domingo (doh-MEEN-goh)

sure adj. seguro (say-GOO-roh)

sweater n. suéter (SWAY-tayr)

sweet adj. dulce (DOOL-say)

swim v. nadar (nah-DAHR)

swimming pool n. piscina; *Mex.* alberca (pee-SEE-nah; ahl-BAYR-cah)

system n. sistema (sees-TAY-mah)

T

table n. mesa (MAY-sah)

tail n. cola (COH-lah)

take v. tomar; llevar (toh-MAHR; yay-VAHR)

take away v. quitar (key-TAHR)

take care of v. cuidar (coo-ee-DAHR)

take off v. quitar(se) (key-TAHR-say)

talk v. hablar (ah-BLAHR)

tall adj. alto (AHL-toh)

tasty adj. sabroso; rico (sah-BROH-soh; REE-coh)

tax n. impuesto (eem-PWAYS-toh)

taxi n. taxi; *Arg.* tacho; *Cuba* máquina (TAHK-see; TAH-choh; MAH-key-nah)

tea n. té (tay)

teach v. enseñar (ayn-say-NYAHR)

team n. equipo (ay-KEY-poh)

technical adj. técnico (TAYK-nee-coh)

telegram n. telegrama (tay-lay-GRAH-mah)

telephone n. teléfono; v. llamar por teléfono (tay-LAY-foh-noh; yah-MAHR pohr tay-LAY-foh-noh)

telephone directory n. guía; *Mex.* directorio telefónico (GHEE-ah; dee-rayk-TOH-ree-oh tay-lay-FOH-nee-coh)

temperature n. temperatura; (med.) fiebre; *Mex.* calentura (taym-pay-rah-TOO-rah; fee-AY-bray; cah-layn-TOO-rah)

ten n., adj. diez (dee-AYS)

tennis n. tenis (TAY-nees)

tent n. tienda de campaña (tee-AYN-dah day cahm-PAH-nyah)

terrible adj. terrible (tay-REE-blay)

than conj. que (kay)

Thank you. Gracias. (GRAH-see-ahs)

That's it! ¡Eso es! (ESS-oh ays)

the art. el, la, los, las (el; lah; lohs; lahs)

theater n. teatro (tay-AH-troh)

their adj. su (soo)

then adv. entonces (ayn-TOHN-says)

there adv. allí (ah-EE)

they pron. ellos (AY-yohs)

thief n. ladrón (lah-DROHN)

thin adj. delgado (dayl-GAH-doh)

thing n. cosa (COH-sah)

think v. pensar (payn-SAHR)

thirteen n., adj. trece (TRAY-say)

thirty n., adj. treinta (TRAYN-tah)

thousand n., adj. mil (meel)

three n., adj. tres (trays)

throat n. garganta (gahr-GHAN-tah)

Thursday n. jueves (hoo-WAY-vays)

ticket n. boleto; *Bol.* entrada (boh-LAY-toh; ayn-TRAH-dah)

tie n. corbata (cohr-BAH-tah)

tile n. azulejo (ah-SOO-lay-hoh)

till prep. hasta; conj. hasta que (AH-stah kay)

time n. tiempo; hora (of day) (tee-AYM-poh; OH-rah)

tip n. propina (proh-PEE-nah)

tire n. llanta; *Chi., Uru.* neumático; *Cuba* goma (YAHN-tah; nay-oo-MAH-tee-coh; GOH-mah)

tired adj. cansado (cahn-SAH-doh)

to prep. a (ah)

tobacco n. tabaco (tah-BAH-coh)

today adv. hoy (oy)

toe n. dedo del pie (DAY-doh dayl pee-AY)

toilet n. inodoro (een-oh-DOH-roh)

toll n. tarifa (tah-REE-fah)

tomato n. tomate; *Mex.* jitomate (toh-MAH-tay; hee-toh-MAH-tay)

tomorrow adv. mañana (mah-NYAH-nah)

tonight n., adv. esta noche (ESS-tah NOH-chay)

too adv. también (tahm-bee-AYN)

too much adv. demasiado (day-mah-see-AH-doh)

tooth n. diente; muela (dee-AYN-tay; moo-AY-lah)

toothache n. dolor de muela (doh-LOHR day moo-AY-lah)

towel n. toalla (toh-AH-yah)

town n. pueblo (PWAY-bloh)

traffic n. tráfico (TRAH-fee-coh)

train n. tren (trayn)

translate v. traducir (trah-doo-CEER)

translation n. traducción (trah-dook-see-OHN)

travel v. viajar (vee-ah-HAHR)

trip n. viaje (vee-AH-hay)

truck n. camión (cah-mee-OHN)

true adj. verdadero (vayr-dah-DAY-roh)

trunk n. baúl (chest) (bah-OOL)

try v. probar; intentar (proh-BAHR; een-tayn-TAHR)

try on v. probar(se) (proh-BAHR-say)

Tuesday n. martes (MAHR-tays)

turn off v. apagar (ah-pah-GAHR)

turn on v. encender (ayn-sayn-DAYR)

twelve n., adj. doce (DOH-say)

twenty n., adj. veinte (VAYN-tay)

two n., adj. dos (dohs)

typical adj. típico (TEE-pee-coh)

U

ugly adj. feo (FAY-oh)

umbrella n. paraguas (pah-RAH-gwahs)

uncomfortable adj. incómodo (een-COH-moh-doh)

under prep. debajo de (day-BAH-hoh day)

underneath adv. debajo (day-BAH-hoh)

understand v. comprender (cohm-prayn-DAYR)

understanding n. entendimiento (ayn-tayn-dee-mee-AYN-toh)

underwear n. ropa interior (ROH-pah een-tay-ree-OHR)

union n. sindicato (trade) (seen-dee-CAH-toh)

university n. universidad (oo-nee-vahr-see-DAHD)

unless conj. a menos (de) que (ah MAY-nohs day kay)

unmarried adj. soltero (sohl-TAY-roh)

unoccupied adj. desocupado (days-oh-coo-PAH-doh)

unpleasant adj. desagradable (days-ah-grah-DAH-blay)

until prep. hasta; conj. hasta que (AH-stah kay)

up adv. arriba (ah-REE-bah)

upon prep. sobre (SOH-bray)

urban adj. urbano (oor-BAH-noh)

urgent adj. urgente (oor-HAYN-tay)

us pron. nos; nosotros (nohs; noh-SOH-trohs)

use n. uso (OO-soh)

use v. usar (oo-SAHR)

useful adj. útil (OO-teel)

usual adj. usual (oo-soo-AHL)

V

vacancy n. vacancia (vah-CAHN-see-ah)

valid adj. válido (VAH-lee-doh)

valley n. valle (VAH-yay)

valuable adj. valioso (vah-lee-OH-soh)

valuables n. objetos de valor (ohb-HAY-tohs day vah-LOHR)

value n. valor (vah-LOHR)

vanilla n. vainilla (vah-ee-NEE-yah)

various adj. varios (VAH-ree-ohs)

veal n. ternera (tayr-NAY-rah)

vegetable n., adj. vegetal (vay-hay-TAHL)

vendor v. vendedor (vayn-day-DOHR)

very adv. muy (MOO-ee)

view n. vista (VEE-stah)

visa n. visa (VEE-sah)

visit v. visitar (vee-see-TAHR)

visitor n. visitante (vee-see-TAHN-tay)

voice n. voz (vohs)

vomit v. vomitar (voh-mee-TAHR)

W

wages n. sueldo (SWAYL-doh)

wait v. esperar (ess-pay-RAHR)

waiter n. mozo; *Cuba* camarero; *Mex.* mesero (MOH-soh; cah-mah-RAY-roh; may-SAY-roh)

wait for v. esperar (ess-pay-RAHR)

waitress n. *Cuba* camarera; *Mex.* mesera (cah-mah-RAY-rah; may-SAY-rah)

walk v. caminar (cah-mee-NAHR)

wall n. pared (pah-RAYD)

wallet n. billetera (bee-yay-TAY-rah)

want v. desear; querer (day-say-AHR; kay-RAYR)

warehouse n. almacén; bodega (ahl-may-SAYN; boh-DAY-gah)

warm adj. caliente (cah-lee-AYN-tay)

wash v. lavar(se) (lah-VAHR-say)

watch n. reloj; v. mirar (ray-LOH; mee-RAHR)

water n. agua (AH-gwah)

we pron. nosotros (noh-SOH-trohs)

weak adj. débil (DAY-beel)

weapon n. arma (AHR-mah)

wear v. llevar (yay-VAHR)

weary adj. cansado (cahn-SAH-doh)

weather n. tiempo (tee-AYM-poh)

Wednesday n. miércoles (mee-AYR-coh-lays)

week n. semana (say-MAH-nah)

weekday n. día laborable (DEE-ah lah-bohr-AH-blay)

weekend n. fin de semana (feen day say-MAH-nah)

weight n. peso (PAY-soh)

welcome adj. bienvenido (bee-ayn-vay-NEE-doh)

well adj., adv. bien (bee-AYN)

well done adj. bien cocido (bee-AYN coh-SEE-doh)

west n. oeste (oh-AY-stay)

what interr. ¿qué?; pron. lo que (kay; loh kay)

whatever adj. cualquier; pron. cualquiera (kwal-key-AYR; kwal-key-AY-rah)

167

wheel n. rueda (roo-AY-dah)

when adv. cuando; interr. ¿cuándo? (KWAN-doh)

where adv. donde; conj. donde; interr. ¿dónde? (DOHN-day)

whether conj. si (see)

while conj. mientras que (mee-AYN-trahs kay)

whisky n. whisky

white n., adj. blanco (BLAHN-coh)

who pron. quien; el que; interr. ¿quién? (key-AYN; el kay)

whole adj. entero (ayn-TAY-roh)

wholesale adj., adv. al por major (ahl pohr mah-YOHR)

why interr. ¿por qué? (pohr kay)

wide adj. ancho (AHN-choh)

width n. ancho (AHN-choh)

wife n. esposa (ess-POH-sah)

win v. ganar (gah-NAHR)

wind n. viento; aire (vee-AYN-toh; AY-ray)

window n. ventana (vayn-TAH-nah)

wine n. vino (VEE-noh)

wineglass n. copa (COH-pah)

winter n. invierno (een-vee-AYR-noh)

wish v. desear; querer (day-say-AHR; kay-RAYR)

witchcraft n. brujería (broo-hay-REE-ah)

with prep. con (cohn)

without prep. sin (seen)

woman n. mujer (moo-HAYR)

wood n. madera (mah-DAY-rah)

wool n. lana (LAH-nah)

word n. palabra (pah-LAH-brah)

work n. trabajo; v. trabajar (trah-BAH-hoh; trah-bah-HAHR)

world n. mundo (MOON-doh)

worry v. preocupar(se) (pray-oh-coo-PAHR-say)

worse adj., adv. peor (pay-OHR)

write v. escribir (ess-cree-VEER)

writer n. escritor (ess-cree-TOHR)

wrong adj. equivocado (ay-key-voh-CAH-doh)

X

X-ray n. rayos X (RAH-yohs AYK-ees)

xylophone n. xilófono (see-LOH-foh-noh)

Y

yacht n. yate (YAH-tay)

year n. año (AHN-yoh)

yearly adj. anual (ah-noo-AHL)

yellow n., adj. amarillo (ah-mah-REE-yoh)

yes adv. sí (see)

yesterday adv. ayer (ay-YAYR)

yet adv. aún; todavía; conj. sin embargo (ah-OON;
    toh-dah-VEE-ah; seen aym-BAHR-goh)

you pron. tú; usted; ustedes (too; oo-STAY;
    oo-STAY-days)

young adj. joven (HOH-vayn)

youngster n. joven (HOH-vayn)

your adj. su; tu (soo; too)

Z

zero n. cero (SAY-roh)

zipper n. *CA, Cuba* zipper; *Mex., Uru.* cierre
    (SEE-payr; see-AY-ray)

zone n. zona (SOH-nah)

zoo n. zoológico (soh-LOH-hee-coh)